MUSIC AT NIGHT

Music At Night

AND OTHER ESSAYS

By Aldous Huxley

Essay Index Reprint Series

 BOOKS FOR LIBRARIES PRESS
FREEPORT, NEW YORK

Copyright © 1931 by Aldous Huxley

Copyright © renewed 1958 by Aldous Huxley

All rights reserved

Reprinted 1970 by arrangement with
Harper & Row, Publishers, Inc.

INTERNATIONAL STANDARD BOOK NUMBER:
0-8369-1960-2

LIBRARY OF CONGRESS CATALOG CARD NUMBER:
77-134098

PRINTED IN THE UNITED STATES OF AMERICA

CONTENTS

SECTION I

Tragedy and the Whole Truth   3
The Rest Is Silence   17
Art and the Obvious   21
'And Wanton Optics Roll the Melting Eye'   30
Music at Night   40
Meditation on El Greco   49

SECTION II

Meditation in Arundel Street   65
Meditation on the Moon   68
On Grace   74
Squeak and Gibber   89
Beliefs and Actions   98
Notes on Liberty and the Boundaries of the Promised Land   107
On the Charms of History and the Future of the Past   119

CONTENTS

SECTION III

Obstacle Race   139
To the Puritan All Things Are Impure   153
Document   163
Points of View   165
Ethics in Andalusia   168

SECTION IV

Foreheads Villainous Low   179
The New Romanticism   188
Selected Snobberies   197
The Beauty Industry   203
Those Personal Touches   211
Wanted, A New Pleasure   221
Sermons in Cats   230

SECTION V

Vulgarity in Literature   243

SECTION I

TRAGEDY
AND THE WHOLE TRUTH

THERE were six of them, the best and bravest of the hero's companions. Turning back from his post in the bows, Odysseus was in time to see them lifted, struggling, into the air, to hear their screams, the desperate repetition of his own name. The survivors could only look on, helplessly, while Scylla 'at the mouth of her cave devoured them, still screaming, still stretching out their hands to me in the frightful struggle.' And Odysseus adds that it was the most dreadful and lamentable sight he ever saw in all his 'explorings of the passes of the sea.' We can believe it; Homer's brief description (the too poetical simile is a later interpolation) convinces us.

Later, the danger passed, Odysseus and his men went ashore for the night, and, on the Sicilian beach, prepared their supper—prepared it, says Homer, 'expertly.'

The Twelfth Book of the *Odyssey* concludes with these words: 'When they had satisfied their thirst and hunger, they thought of their dear companions and wept, and in the midst of their tears sleep came gently upon them.'

The truth, the whole truth and nothing but the truth —how rarely the older literatures ever told it! Bits of the truth, yes; every good book gives us bits of the truth, would not be a good book if it did not. But the whole truth, no. Of the great writers of the past incredibly few have given us that. Homer—the Homer of the *Odyssey*—is one of those few.

'Truth?' you question. 'For example, 2+2=4? Or Queen Victoria came to the throne in 1837? Or light travels at the rate of 187,000 miles a second?' No, obviously, you won't find much of that sort of thing in literature. The 'truth' of which I was speaking just now is in fact no more than an acceptable verisimilitude. When the experiences recorded in a piece of literature correspond fairly closely with our own actual experiences, or with what I may call our potential experiences —experiences, that is to say, which we feel (as the result of a more or less explicit process of inference from known facts) that we might have had—we say, inaccurately no doubt: 'This piece of writing is true.' But this, of course, is not the whole story. The record of a case in a text-book of psychology is scientifically true, in so far as it is an accurate account of particular events. But it might also strike the reader as being 'true' with regard to himself—that is to say, acceptable, probable, having a correspondence with his own actual or potential experiences. But a text-book of psychology is not a work of art—or only secondarily and incidentally a work of art. Mere verisimilitude, mere correspondence of experience recorded by the writer with experience remembered or imaginable by the reader, is not enough to make a work of art seem 'true.' Good art possesses a kind of super-truth—is more probable, more acceptable, more convincing than fact itself. Naturally; for the artist is endowed with a sensibility and a power of communication, a capacity to 'put things across,' which events and the majority of people to whom events happen, do not possess. Experience teaches only the teachable, who are by no means as numerous as Mrs. Micawber's papa's favourite proverb would lead us to suppose. Artists are eminently teachable and also eminently teachers. They receive from events much more than most men receive and they can transmit what they have received with a peculiar penetrative force, which drives their communication deep into the reader's mind. One of our most ordinary reactions to a good piece of literary art is expressed in the formula: 'This is what I have always felt and thought, but have never been able to put clearly into words, even for myself.'

We are now in a position to explain what we mean, when we say that Homer is a writer who tells the Whole Truth. We mean that the experiences he records correspond fairly closely with our own actual or potential experiences—and correspond with our experiences not on a single limited sector, but all along the line of our physical and spiritual being. And we also mean that Homer records these experiences with a penetrative artistic force that makes them seem peculiarly acceptable and convincing.

So much, then, for truth in literature. Homer's, I repeat, is the Whole Truth. Consider how almost any other of the great poets would have concluded the story of Scylla's attack on the passing ship. Six men, remember, have been taken and devoured before the eyes of their friends. In any other poem but the *Odyssey*, what would the survivors have done? They would, of course, have wept, even as Homer made them weep. But would they previously have cooked their supper, and cooked it, what's more, in a masterly fashion? Would they previously have drunk and eaten to satiety? And after weeping, or actually while weeping, would they have dropped quietly off to sleep? No, they most certainly would not have done any of these things.

They would simply have wept, lamenting their own misfortune and the horrible fate of their companions, and the Canto would have ended tragically on their tears.

Homer, however, preferred to tell the Whole Truth. He knew that even the most cruelly bereaved must eat; that hunger is stronger than sorrow and that its satisfaction takes precedence even of tears. He knew that experts continue to act expertly and to find satisfaction in their accomplishment, even when friends have just been eaten, even when the accomplishment is only cooking the supper. He knew that, when the belly is full (and only when the belly is full), men can afford to grieve, and that sorrow after supper is almost a luxury. And finally he knew that, even as hunger takes precedence of grief, so fatigue, supervening, cuts short its career and drowns it in a sleep all the sweeter for bringing forgetfulness of bereavement. In a word, Homer refused to treat the theme tragically. He preferred to tell the Whole Truth.

Another author who preferred to tell the Whole Truth was Fielding. *Tom Jones* is one of the very few Odyssean books written in Europe between the time of Aeschylus and the present age; Odyssean, because never tragical; never—even when painful and disastrous, even when pathetic and beautiful things are happening. For they do happen; Fielding, like Homer, admits all the facts, shirks nothing. Indeed, it is precisely because these authors shirk nothing that their books are not tragical. For among the things they don't shirk are the irrelevancies which, in actual life, always temper the situations and characters that writers of tragedy insist on keeping chemically pure. Consider, for example, the case of Sophy Western, that most charming, most nearly perfect of young women. Fielding, it is obvious, adored her (she is said to have been created in the image of his first, much-loved wife). But in spite of his adoration, he refused to turn her into one of those chemically pure and, as it were, focussed beings who do not suffer in the world of tragedy. That innkeeper who lifted the weary Sophia from her horse—what need had he to fall? In no tragedy would he (nay, *could* he) have collapsed beneath her weight. For, to begin with, in the tragical context weight is an irrelevance; heroines should be above the law of gravitation. But that is not all; let the reader now remember what were the results of his fall. Tumbling flat on his back, he pulled Sophia down on top of him—his belly was a cushion, so that happily she came to no bodily harm—pulled her down head first. But head first is necessarily legs last; there was a momentary display of the most ravishing charms; the bumpkins at the inn door grinned and guffawed; poor Sophia, when they picked her up, was blushing in an agony of embarrassment and wounded modesty. There is nothing intrinsically improbable about this incident, which is stamped, indeed, with all the marks of literary truth. But however true, it is an incident which could never, never have happened to a heroine of tragedy. It would never have been allowed to happen. But Fielding refused to impose the tragedian's veto; he shirked nothing—neither the intrusion of irrelevant absurdities into the midst of romance or disaster, nor any of life's no less irrelevantly painful interruptions of the course of happiness. He did not want to be a tragedian. And, sure enough, that brief and pearly gleam of Sophia's charming posterior was sufficient to scare the Muse of Tragedy out of *Tom Jones* just as, more than five and twenty centuries before, the sight of stricken men first eating, then remembering to weep, then forgetting their tears in slumber had scared her out of the *Odyssey*.

In his *Principles of Literary Criticism* Mr. I. A. Richards affirms that good tragedy is proof against irony and irrelevance—that it can absorb anything into itself and still remain tragedy. Indeed, he seems to make of this capacity to absorb the untragical and the anti-tragical a touchstone of tragic merit. Thus tried, practically all Greek, all French and most Elizabethan tragedies are found wanting. Only the best of Shakespeare can stand the test. So, at least, says Mr. Richards.

Is he right? I have often had my doubts. The tragedies of Shakespeare are veined, it is true, with irony and an often terrifying cynicism; but the cynicism is always heroic idealism turned neatly inside out, the irony is a kind of photographic negative of heroic romance. Turn Troilus's white into black and all his blacks into white and you have Thersites. Reversed, Othello and Desdemona become Iago. White Ophelia's negative is the irony of Hamlet, is the ingenuous bawdry of her own mad songs; just as the cynicism of mad King Lear is the black shadow-replica of Cordelia. Now, the shadow, the photographic negative of a thing is in no sense irrelevant to it. Shakespeare's ironies and cynicisms serve to deepen his tragic world, but not to widen it. If they had widened it, as the Homeric irrelevancies widened out the universe of the *Odyssey*—why, then, the world of Shakespearean tragedy would automatically have ceased to exist. For example, a scene showing the bereaved Macduff eating his supper, growing melancholy, over the whisky, with thoughts of his murdered wife and children, and then, with lashes still wet, dropping off to sleep, would be true enough to life; but it would not be true to tragic art. The introduction of such a scene would change the whole quality of the play; treated in this Odyssean style, *Macbeth* would cease to be a tragedy. Or take the case of Desdemona. Iago's bestially

TRAGEDY AND THE WHOLE TRUTH

cynical remarks about her character are in no sense, as we have seen, irrelevant to the tragedy. They present us with negative images of her real nature and of the feelings she has for Othello. These negative images are always *hers*, are always recognizably the property of the heroine-victim of a tragedy. Whereas, if, springing ashore at Cyprus, she had tumbled, as the no less exquisite Sophia was to tumble, and revealed the inadequacies of sixteenth-century underclothing, the play would no longer be the *Othello* we know. Iago might breed a family of little cynics and the existing dose of bitterness and savage negation be doubled and trebled; *Othello* would still remain fundamentally *Othello*. But a few Fieldingesque irrelevancies would destroy it—destroy it, that is to say, as a tragedy; for there would be nothing to prevent it from becoming a magnificent drama of some other kind. For the fact is that tragedy and what I have called the Whole Truth are not compatible; where one is, the other is not. There are certain things which even the best, even Shakespearean tragedy, cannot absorb into itself.

To make a tragedy the artist must isolate a single element out of the totality of human experience and use that exclusively as his material. Tragedy is something that is separated out from the Whole Truth, distilled from it, so to speak, as an essence is distilled from the living flower. Tragedy is chemically pure. Hence its power to act quickly and intensely on our feelings. All chemically pure art has this power to act upon us quickly and intensely. Thus, chemically pure pornography (on the rare occasions when it happens to be written convincingly, by some one who has the gift of 'putting things across') is a quick-acting emotional drug of incomparably greater power than the Whole Truth about sensuality, or even (for many people) than the tangible and carnal reality itself. It is because of its chemical purity that tragedy so effectively performs its function of catharsis. It refines and corrects and gives a style to our emotional life, and does so swiftly, with power. Brought into contact with tragedy, the elements of our being fall, for the moment at any rate, into an ordered and beautiful pattern, as the iron filings arrange themselves under the influence of the magnet. Through all its individual variations, this pattern is always fundamentally of the same kind. From the reading or the hearing of a tragedy we rise with the feeling that

> *Our friends are exultations, agonies,*
> *And love, and man's unconquerable mind;*

with the heroic conviction that we too would be unconquerable if subjected to the agonies, that in the midst of the agonies we too should continue to love, might even learn to exult. It is because it does these things to us that tragedy is felt to be so valuable. What are the values of Wholly-Truthful art? What does it do to us that seems worth doing? Let us try to discover.

Wholly-Truthful art overflows the limits of tragedy and shows us, if only by hints and implications, what happened before the tragic story began, what will happen after it is over, what is happening simultaneously elsewhere (and 'elsewhere' includes all those parts of the minds and bodies of the protagonists not immediately engaged in the tragic struggle). Tragedy is an arbitrarily isolated eddy on the surface of a vast river that flows on majestically, irresistibly, around, beneath, and to either side of it. Wholly-Truthful art contrives to imply the existence of the entire river as well as of the eddy. It is quite different from tragedy, even though it may contain, among other constituents, all the elements from which tragedy is made. (The 'same thing' placed in different contexts, loses its identity and becomes, for the perceiving mind, a succession of different things.) In Wholly-Truthful art the agonies may be just as real, love and the unconquerable mind just as admirable, just as important, as in tragedy. Thus, Scylla's victims suffer as painfully as the monster-devoured Hippolytus in *Phèdre;* the mental anguish of Tom Jones when he thinks he has lost his Sophia, and lost her by his own fault, is hardly less than that of Othello after Desdemona's murder. (The fact that Fielding's power of 'putting things across' is by no means equal to Shakespeare's, is, of course, merely an accident.) But the agonies and indomitabilities are placed by the Wholly-Truthful writer in another, wider context, with the result that they cease to be the same as the intrinsically identical agonies and indomitabilities of tragedy. Consequently, Wholly-Truthful art produces in us an effect quite different from that produced by tragedy. Our mood, when we have read a Wholly-Truthful book, is never one of heroic exultation; it is one of resignation, of acceptance. (Acceptance can also be heroic.) Being chemically impure, Wholly-Truthful literature cannot move us as quickly and intensely as tragedy or any other kind of chemically pure art. But I believe that its effects are more lasting. The exultations that follow the reading or hearing of a tragedy are in the nature of temporary inebriations. Our being cannot long hold the pattern imposed by tragedy. Remove the magnet and the filings tend to fall back into confusion. But the pattern of acceptance and resignation imposed upon us by Wholly-Truthful literature, though perhaps less unexpectedly beautiful in design, is (for that very reason perhaps) more stable.

The catharsis of tragedy is violent and apocalyptic; but the milder catharsis of Wholly-Truthful literature is lasting.

In recent times literature has become more and more acutely conscious of the Whole Truth—of the great oceans of irrelevant things, events and thoughts stretching endlessly away in every direction from whatever island point (a character, a story) the author may choose to contemplate. To impose the kind of arbitrary limitations, which must be imposed by any one who wants to write a tragedy, has become more and more difficult—is now indeed, for those who are at all sensitive to contemporaneity, almost impossible. This does not mean, of course, that the modern writer must confine himself to a merely naturalistic manner. One can imply the existence of the Whole Truth without laboriously cataloguing every object within sight. A book can be written in terms of pure phantasy and yet, by implication, tell the Whole Truth. Of all the important works of contemporary literature not one is a pure tragedy. There is no contemporary writer of significance who does not prefer to state or imply the Whole Truth. However different one from another in style, in ethical, philosophical and artistic intention, in the scales of values accepted, contemporary writers have this in common, that they are interested in the Whole Truth.

Proust, D. H. Lawrence, André Gide, Kafka, Hemingway—here are five obviously significant and important contemporary writers. Five authors as remarkably unlike one another as they could well be. They are at one only in this: that none of them has written a pure tragedy, that all are concerned with the Whole Truth.

I have sometimes wondered whether tragedy, as a form of art, may not be doomed. But the fact that we are still profoundly moved by the tragic masterpieces of the past—that we can be moved, against our better judgment, even by the bad tragedies of the contemporary stage and film—makes me think that the day of chemically pure art is not over. Tragedy happens to be passing through a period of eclipse, because all the significant writers of our age are too busy exploring the newly discovered, or re-discovered, world of the Whole Truth to be able to pay any attention to it. But there is no good reason to believe that this state of things will last for ever. Tragedy is too valuable to be allowed to die. There is no reason, after all, why the two kinds of literature—the Chemically Impure and the Chemically Pure, the literature of the Whole Truth and the literature of Partial Truth—should not exist simultaneously, each in its separate sphere. The human spirit has need of both.

THE REST IS SILENCE

FROM pure sensation to the intuition of beauty, from pleasure and pain to love and the mystical ecstasy and death—all the things that are fundamental, all the things that, to the human spirit, are most profoundly significant can only be experienced, not expressed. The rest is always and everywhere silence.

After silence that which comes nearest to expressing the inexpressible is music. (And, significantly, silence is an integral part of all good music. Compared with Beethoven's or Mozart's, the ceaseless torrent of Wagner's music is very poor in silence. Perhaps that is one of the reasons why it seems so much less significant than theirs. It 'says' less because it is always speaking.)

In a different mode, on another plane of being, music is the equivalent of some of man's most significant and most inexpressible experiences. By mysterious analogy it evokes in the mind of the listener, sometimes the phantom of these experiences, sometimes even the experiences themselves in their full force of life—it is a question of intensity; the phantom is dim, the reality, near and burning. Music may call up either; it is chance or providence which decides. The intermittences of the heart are subject to no known law. Another peculiarity of music is its capacity (shared to some extent by all the other arts) to evoke experiences as perfect wholes (perfect and whole, that is to say, in respect to each listener's capacity to have any given experience), however partial, however obscurely confused may have been the originals thus recalled. We are grateful to the artist, especially the musician, for 'saying clearly what we have always felt, but never been able to express.' Listening to expressive music, we have, not of course the artist's original experience (which is quite beyond us, for grapes do not grow on thistles), but the best experience in its kind of which our nature is capable—a better and completer experience than in fact we ever had before listening to the music.

Music's ability to express the inexpressible was recognized by the greatest of all verbal artists. The man who wrote *Othello* and *The Winter's Tale* was capable of uttering in words whatever words can possibly be made to signify. And yet (I am indebted here to a very interesting essay by Mr. Wilson Knight) and yet whenever something in the nature of a mystical emotion or intuition had to be communicated, Shakespeare regularly called upon music to help him to 'put it across.' My own infinitesimally small experience of theatrical production convinces me that, if he chose his music well, he need never have called upon it in vain.

In the last act of the play which was drawn from my novel, *Point Counter Point*, selections from the slow movement of the Beethoven A minor quartet take their place as an integral part of the drama. Neither the play nor the music is mine; so that I am at liberty to say that the effect of the *Heilige Dankgesang*, when actually played during the performance, was to my mind, at least, prodigious.

'Had we but world enough and time . . .' But those are precisely the things that the theatre cannot give us. From the abbreviated play it was necessary to omit almost all the implied or specified 'counter' which, in the novel, tempered, or at least was intended to temper, the harshness of the 'points.' The play, as a whole, was curiously hard and brutal. Bursting suddenly into this world of almost unmitigated harshness, the *Heilige Dankgesang* seemed like the manifestation of something supernatural. It was as though a god had really and visibly descended, awful and yet reassuring, mysteriously wrapped in the peace that passes all understanding, divinely beautiful.

My novel might have been the Book of Job and its adapter, Mr. Campbell Dixon, the author of *Macbeth;* but whatever our capacities, whatever pains we might have taken, we should have found it absolutely impossible to express by means of words or dramatic action what those three or four minutes of violin playing made somehow so luminously manifest to any sensitive listener.

When the inexpressible had to be expressed, Shakespeare laid down his pen and called for music. And if the music should also fail? Well, there was always silence to fall back on. For always, always and everywhere, the rest is silence.

ART AND THE OBVIOUS

ALL great truths are obvious truths. But not all obvious truths are great truths. Thus it is to the last degree obvious that life is short and destiny uncertain. It is obvious that, to a great extent, happiness depends on oneself and not on external circumstances. It is obvious that parents generally love their children and that men and women are attracted one to another in a variety of ways. It is obvious that many people enjoy the country and are moved by the varying aspects of nature to feel elation, awe, tenderness, gaiety, melancholy. It is obvious that most men and women are attached to their homes and countries, to the beliefs which they were taught in childhood and the moral code of their tribe. All these, I repeat, are obvious truths and all are great truths, because they are universally significant, because they refer to fundamental characteristics of human nature.

But there is another class of obvious truths—the obvious truths which, lacking eternal significance and having no reference to the fundamentals of human nature, cannot be called great truths. Thus, it is obvious to any one who has ever been there or even remotely heard of the place, that there are a great many automobiles in New York and a number of very lofty buildings. It is obvious that evening frocks are longer this year and that very few men wear top hats or high starched collars. It is obvious that you can fly from London to Paris in two and a half hours, that there is a periodical called the *Saturday Evening Post*, that the earth is round, and that Mr. Wrigley makes chewing-gum. In spite of their obviousness, at any rate at the present time—for a time may come when evening frocks, whether long or short, will not be worn at all and when the motor car will be a museum curiosity, like the machines in *Erewhon* —these truths are not great truths. They might cease to be true without human nature being in the least changed in any of its fundamentals.

Popular art makes use, at the present time, of both classes of obvious truths—of the little obviousnesses as well as of the great. Little obviousnesses fill (at a moderate computation) quite half of the great majority of contemporary novels, stories, and films. The great public derives an extraordinary pleasure from the mere recognition of familiar objects and circumstances. It tends to be somewhat disquieted by works of pure phantasy, whose subject-matter is drawn from other worlds than that in which it lives, moves, and has its daily being. Films must have plenty of real Ford cars and genuine policemen and indubitable trains. Novels must contain long descriptions of exactly those rooms, those streets, those restaurants and shops and offices with which the average man and woman are most familiar. Each reader, each member of the audience must be able to say—with what a solid satisfaction!—'Ah, there's a real Ford, there's a policeman, that's a drawing-room exactly like the Browns' drawing-room.' Recognizableness is an artistic quality which most people find profoundly thrilling.

Nor are small obvious truths the only obviousnesses appreciated by the public at large. It also demands the great obvious truths. It demands from the purveyors of art the most definite statements as to the love of mothers for children, the goodness of honesty as a policy, the uplifting effects produced by the picturesque beauties of nature on tourists from large cities, the superiority of marriages of affection to marriages of interest, the brevity of human existence, the beauty of first love and so forth. It requires a constantly repeated assurance of the validity of these great obvious truths. And the purveyors of popular art do what is asked of them. They state the great, obvious, unchanging truths of human nature—but state them, alas, in most cases with an emphatic incompetence, which, to the sensitive reader, makes their affirmations exceedingly distasteful and even painful. Thus, the fact that mothers love their children is, as I have pointed out, one of the great obvious truths. But when this great obvious truth is affirmed in a nauseatingly treacly mammy-song, in a series of soulful close-ups, in a post-Wilcoxian lyric or a page of magazine-story prose, the sensitive can only wince and avert their faces, blushing with a kind of vicarious shame for the whole of humanity.

The great obvious truths have often, in the past, been stated with a repellent emphasis, in tones that made them seem—for such is the almost magical power of artistic incompetence—not great truths, but great and frightful lies. But never in the past have these artistic outrages been so numerous as at present. This is due to several causes. To begin with, the spread of education, of leisure, of economic well-being has created an unprecedented demand for popular art. As the number of good artists is always strictly limited, it follows that this demand has been in the main supplied by bad artists.

Hence the affirmations of the great obvious truths have been in general incompetent and therefore odious. It is possible, also, that the break-up of all the old traditions, the mechanization of work and leisure (from both of which creative effort has now, for the vast majority of civilized men and women, been banished), have had a bad effect on popular taste and popular emotional sensibility. But in any case, whatever the causes, the fact remains that the present age has produced a hitherto unprecedented quantity of popular art (popular in the sense that it is made *for* the people, but not—and this is the modern tragedy—*by* the people), and that this popular art is composed half of the little obvious truths, stated generally with a careful and painstaking realism, half of the great obvious truths, stated for the most part (since it is very hard to give them satisfactory expression) with an incompetence, which makes them seem false and repellent.

On some of the most sensitive and self-conscious artists of our age, this state of affairs has had a curious and, I believe, unprecedented effect. They have become afraid of all obviousness, the great as well as the little. At every period, it is true, many artists have been afraid—or, perhaps it would be more accurate to say, have been contemptuous—of the little obvious truths. In the history of the arts naturalism is a relatively rare phenomenon; judged by any standard of statistical normality, Caravaggio and the Victorian academician were artistic freaks. The unprecedented fact is this: some of the most sensitive artists of our age have rejected not merely external realism (for which we may be rather thankful), but even what I may call internal realism; they refuse to take cognizance in their art of most of the most significant facts of human nature. The excesses of popular art have filled them with a terror of the obvious—even of the obvious sublimities and beauties and marvels. Now, about nine-tenths of life are made up precisely of the obvious. Which means that there are sensitive modern artists who are compelled, by their disgust and fear, to confine themselves to the exploitation of only a tiny fraction of existence.

The most self-conscious of contemporary artistic centres is Paris, and it is, as we should expect, in Paris that this strange new fear of the obvious has borne the most striking fruits. But what is true of Paris is also true of the other artistic capitals of the world. Either because they are deliberately imitating French models, or else because they have been driven by similar circumstances to make a similar reaction. The advanced art of other countries differs from the advanced art of France only in being rather less deliberate and less thorough-going. In every country, but in France a little more clearly than elsewhere, we see how the same fear of the obvious has produced the same effects. We see the plastic arts stripped of all their 'literary' qualities, pictures and statues reduced to their strictly formal elements. We listen to a music from which almost every expression of a tragical, a mournful, a tender sentiment has been excluded—a music that has deliberately confined itself to the expression of physical energy, of the lyricism of speed and mechanical motion. Both music and the visual arts are impregnated to a greater or less extent with that new topsy-turvy romanticism, which exalts the machine, the crowd, the merely muscular body, and despises the soul and solitude and nature. Advanced literature is full of the same reversed romanticism. Its subject-matter is arbitrarily simplified by the exclusion of all the great eternal obviousnesses of human nature. This process is justified theoretically by a kind of philosophy of history which affirms—quite gratuitously and, I am convinced, quite falsely—that human nature has radically changed in the last few years and that the modern man is, or at least ought to be, radically different from his ancestors. Nor is it only in regard to subject-matter that the writer's fear of the obvious manifests itself. He has a terror of the obvious in his artistic medium—a terror which leads him to make laborious efforts to destroy the gradually perfected instrument of language. Those who are completely and ruthlessly logical parade a total nihilism and would like to see the abolition of all art, all science, and all organized society whatsoever. It is extraordinary to what lengths a panic fear can drive its victims.

Almost all that is most daring in contemporary art is thus seen to be the fruit of terror—the terror, in an age of unprecedented vulgarity, of the obvious. The spectacle of so much fear-inspired boldness is one which I find rather depressing. If young artists really desire to offer proof of their courage they should attack the monster of obviousness and try to conquer it, try to reduce it to a state of artistic domestication, not timorously run away from it. For the great obvious truths are there—facts. Those who deny their existence, those who proclaim that human nature has changed since August 4, 1914, are merely rationalizing their terrors and disgusts. Popular art gives a deplorably beastly expression to the obvious; sensitive men and women hate this beastly expression; therefore, by a natural but highly unscientific process, they affirm that the things so hatefully expressed do not exist. But they do exist, as any dispassionate survey of the facts makes clear. And since they exist, they should be faced, fought with, and reduced to artistic order. By pretending that certain things are not there, which in fact *are* there, much of the most accomplished modern art is condemning itself to incompleteness, to sterility, to premature decrepitude and death.

'AND WANTON OPTICS ROLL THE MELTING EYE'

The sunrise was magnificent. The luminary of day, like a disc of metal gilded by the Tuolz process, came up from the Ocean, as from an immense voltaic bath. JULES VERNE.

POETRY and Science: a marriage has been arranged—again and again, in the minds of how many ambitious young men of letters! But either the engagement was broken off; or else, if consummated, the marriage was fertile only of abortions. Education, The Sugar Cane, The Loves of the Plants, Cyder, The Fleece—their forgotten names are legion.

On what conditions is the marriage possible? Let Wordsworth answer. 'The remotest discoveries of the chemist, the botanist, or the mineralogist, will be as proper objects of the poet's art as any upon which he is now employed, if the time should ever come when these things shall be manifestly and palpably material to us as enjoying and suffering beings.' Poetry can be made out of science, but only when the contemplation of scientific facts has modified the pattern, not only of the poet's intellectual beliefs, but of his spiritual existence as a whole—his 'inscape,' as Father Hopkins calls it. Information which has modified the poet's existence-pattern may be expected (when skilfully 'put across' in terms of art) to modify the existence-pattern of his reader. In good scientific poetry the science is there, not primarily for its own sake, but because it is a modifier of existence-pattern. Bad scientific poetry is of two kinds: that in which the science is meant to be a modifier of existence-patterns, but owing to the poet's incompetence as a communicator, fails to do what it was meant to do; and that in which the science is there primarily for its own sake, and not to produce an effect on existence-patterns. Most professedly didactic poems are of this type.

> *Gnomes, as you now dissect with hammers fine*
> *The granite rock, the noduled flint calcine;*
> *Grind with strong arm the circling Chertz betwixt,*
> *Your pure Kaolin and Petuntses mixt.*

The scientific information contained by implication in these lines would be much more effectively communicated in the prose of a geological text-book. Text-book prose exists for the purpose of imparting information as accurately as possible. To inform is only a secondary function of poetical language, which exists primarily as an instrument for the modification of existence-patterns.

Information about kaolin is not likely to modify the existence-pattern of any normally constituted human being, however learned in geology—though of course a lyrical poet who happened to be so learned might use a fact about kaolin to illuminate a wholly non-geological theme. The universally knowledgeable Donne made use of the most 'remote discoveries' of the scientists of his time as illustrations and enrichments. Kaolin, or its equivalents, helped him to 'put across' what he felt about love, God, death, and many other pattern-modifying matters. It was as a suffering and enjoying man that he made use of his knowledge. The didactic poets, on the contrary, were, in almost all cases, primarily students. 'The Botanic Garden' and 'The Economy of Vegetation' provide no internal evidence to show that Erasmus Darwin's general 'inscape' was modified by what he had learnt about kaolin and the like.

There is much rhymed astronomy in the *Divine Comedy;* but it is never, like Erasmus Darwin's rhymed botany and rhymed geology, ridiculous. Why is this? In the first place, Dante had an incomparable capacity for 'putting things across.' And in the second place, that which he put across was not merely scientific information; it was always scientific information that had modified the pattern of Dante's whole existence. 'An infidel astronomer is mad.' For Dante, it is evident, the heavens (the ptolemaic heavens in all their intricate detail of sphere and epicycle) proclaimed the glory of God. The most unlikely piece of information about the sun or the stars was never merely a piece of out-of-the-way information; it was indissolubly a part of that religious system which patterned the whole of Dante's existence. Most of us are ignorant where Dante was learned and sceptical about what he believed. Consequently, in such lines as—

> *Surge ai mortali per diverse foci*
> *la lucerna del mondo; ma da quella,*
> *che quattro cerchi giunge con tre croci,*
> *con miglior corso e con migliore stella*
> *esce congiunta.*

we are struck only by the musically perfect language and a certain oracular obscurity of utterance, intrinsically poetical (for the musically incomprehensible is always charged with a certain magical power). But this abracadabra of circles and crosses has a scientific meaning, this riddle is a statement of fact. Dante evidently liked conveying information in terms of riddles. Where, as in the present case, the riddling information is about the 'remotest discoveries' of astronomy, no one who does not know it in advance can possibly guess the answer to the enigma. Most of the *Divine Comedy* cannot be fully understood except by those who have a special culture. (The same is true of more or less considerable parts of many other poems.)

Solving riddles is an occupation that appeals to almost all of us. All poetry consists, to a greater or less extent, of riddles, to which the answers are occasionally, as in Dante's case, scientific or metaphysical. One of the pleasures we derive from poetry is precisely the crossword puzzler's delight in working out a problem. For certain people, this pleasure is peculiarly intense. Nature's puzzle solvers, they tend to value poetry in proportion as it is obscure. I have known such people who, too highbrow to indulge in the arduous imbecilities of cross-word and acrostic, sought satisfaction for an imperious yearning in the sonnets of Mallarmé and the more eccentric verses of Gerard Hopkins.

To return to our circles and crosses: when you have sufficiently mugged up the notes to your *Paradiso* you realize that, when he wrote those lines, Dante was saying something extremely definite, and that he must have had before his inward eye a very precise and (what is poetically more important) a grandiose, a deeply impressive picture of the entire ptolemaic universe. Six

'AND WANTON OPTICS' 35

centuries have made of Dante's science (even as Chaucer foresaw that they would make of his own fourteenth-century language) something 'wonder nice and strange.' Past literature is a charnel-house of dead words, past philosophy a mine of fossil facts and theories.

> *And yet they spake them so,*
> *And sped as well in love as men now do.*

Chaucer protested in advance against oblivion. In vain. His speech and Dante's science are dead, forgotten. What readers has the *Divine Comedy* now? A few poets, a few lovers of poetry, a few strayed crossword puzzlers, and, for the rest, a diminishing band of culture-fans and erudition-snobs. These last feel as triumphantly superior in their exclusive learning as would the social snob if, alone of all his acquaintance, he had met the Prince of Wales, or could speak of Mr. Michael Arlen by his pet name. Even in Dante's day the cultured few who knew offhand that *'da quella, che giunge quattro cerchi con tre croci'* was the esoteric pet name of sunrise at the equinox must have felt a certain glow of conscious superiority. Now, six centuries later, these knowledgeable ones are justified in going off into positive raptures of self-satisfaction. Deathless verse dies like all the rest. A good dose of science can be relied on, as we see in Dante's case, to abbreviate its immortality.

An infidel astronomer is mad; but even madder is a believing and practising one. So, at any rate, Lucretius thought. That was why he wanted to convert everyone to science. For most men are sane; convert them, and they will automatically cease to be pious. The spectacle of human life lying 'foully prostrate upon earth, crushed down by the weight of religion,' was something that moved Lucretius to righteous anger. His aim was to destroy the tyrant, to see that religion was 'put under foot and trampled on in turn.' For Dante, the heavens in all their intricacy of detail movingly proclaimed the glory of God; for Lucretius they no less movingly proclaimed God's impersonality, almost His non-existence. To both poets 'the remotest discoveries' of the scientists were profoundly and humanly important. The centuries have passed and the science of Lucretius and Dante is mostly obsolete and untrue. In spite of the ardour and enthusiasm with which they wrote, in spite of their prodigious powers of communication, it is as students primarily, as archæologists, that we now read what they composed as suffering and enjoying beings. Leaving out of account the non-scientific, 'human' parts of the two poems, the only passages in *De Rerum Natura* and the *Divine Comedy* which still move us as their authors meant them to move, are those in which the poets generalize—those in which, by statement or implication, they set forth the hypothesis which their information about 'remote discoveries' is supposed to prove, and proceed to show how this hypothesis, if accepted, must affect our attitude towards the world, modify the pattern of our being. Lucretius's statements of the materialist and Dante's of the spiritualist philosophy still have power to modify our existence-pattern, even though most of the 'facts' on which they based their respective philosophies are now no more than archæological specimens.

The facts and even the peculiar jargon of science can be of great service to the writer whose intention is mainly ironical. Juxtapose two accounts of the same human event, one in terms of pure science, the other in terms of religion, aesthetics, passion, even common sense: their discord will set up the most disquieting reverberations in the mind. Juxtapose, for example, physiology and mysticism (Mme. Guyon's ecstasies were most frequent and most spiritually significant in the fourth month of her pregnancies); juxtapose acoustics and the music of Bach (perhaps I may be permitted to refer to the simultaneously scientific and aesthetic account of a concert in my novel, *Point Counter Point*); juxtapose chemistry and the soul (the ductless glands secrete among other things our moods, our aspirations, our philosophy of life). This list of linked incompatibles might be indefinitely prolonged. We live in a world of *non sequiturs*. Or rather, we would live in such a world, if we were always conscious of all the aspects under which any event can be considered. But in practice, we are almost never aware of more than one aspect of each event at a time. Our life is spent first in one watertight compartment of experience, then in another. The artist can, if he so desires, break down the bulkheads between the compartments and so give us a simultaneous view of two or more of them at a time. So seen, reality looks exceedingly queer. Which is how the ironist and the perplexed questioner desire it to look. Laforgue constantly makes use of this device. All his poetry is a mixture of remote discovery with near sentiment. Hence its pervading quality of irony. In the remote future, when a science infinitely better informed than ours shall have bridged the now enormous gulf between immediately apprehended qualities, in terms of which we *live*, and the merely measurable, ponderable quantities in terms of which we do our scientific thinking, the Laforguian method will cease to be ironical. For the juxtaposition will then be a juxtaposition of compatibles, not of incompatibles. There will be no curious discord, but a perfectly plain and simple harmony. But all this is for the future. So far as we are concerned, the bringing together of remote discoveries and near feelings is productive of literary effects which we recognize as ironical.

MUSIC AT NIGHT

Moonless, this June night is all the more alive with stars. Its darkness is perfumed with faint gusts from the blossoming lime trees, with the smell of wetted earth and the invisible greenness of the vines. There is silence; but a silence that breathes with the soft breathing of the sea and, in the thin shrill noise of a cricket, insistently, incessantly harps on the fact of its own deep perfection. Far away, the passage of a train is like a long caress, moving gently, with an inexorable gentleness, across the warm living body of the night.

Music, you say; it would be a good night for music. But I have music here in a box, shut up, like one of those bottled djinns in the *Arabian Nights*, and ready at a touch to break out of its prison. I make the necessary mechanical magic, and suddenly, by some miraculously appropriate coincidence (for I had selected the record in the dark, without knowing what music the machine would play), suddenly the introduction to the *Benedictus* in Beethoven's *Missa Solemnis* begins to trace its patterns on the moonless sky.

The *Benedictus*. Blessed and blessing, this music is in some sort the equivalent of the night, of the deep and living darkness, into which, now in a single jet, now in a fine interweaving of melodies, now in pulsing and almost solid clots of harmonious sound, it pours itself, stanchlessly pours itself, like time, like the rising and falling, falling trajectories of a life. It is the equivalent of the night in another mode of being, as an essence is the equivalent of the flowers, from which it is distilled.

There is, at least there sometimes seems to be, a certain blessedness lying at the heart of things, a mysterious blessedness, of whose existence occasional accidents or providences (for me, this night is one of them) make us obscurely, or it may be intensely, but always fleetingly, alas, always only for a few brief moments aware. In the *Benedictus* Beethoven gives expression to this awareness of blessedness. His music is the equivalent of this Mediterranean night, or rather of the blessedness at the heart of the night, of the blessedness as it would be if it could be sifted clear of irrelevance and accident, refined and separated out into its quintessential purity.

'*Benedictus, benedictus* . . .' One after another the

voices take up the theme propounded by the orchestra and lovingly meditated through a long and exquisite solo (for the blessedness reveals itself most often to the solitary spirit) by a single violin. '*Benedictus, benedictus* . . .' And then, suddenly, the music dies; the flying djinn has been rebottled. With a stupid insect-like insistence, a steel point rasps and rasps the silence.

. . . . .

At school, when they taught us what was technically known as English, they used to tell us to 'express in our own words' some passage from whatever play of Shakespeare was at the moment being rammed, with all its annotations—particularly the annotations—down our reluctant throats. So there we would sit, a row of inky urchins, laboriously translating 'now silken dalliance in the wardrobe lies' into 'now smart silk clothes lie in the wardrobe,' or 'To be or not to be' into 'I wonder whether I ought to commit suicide or not.' When we had finished, we would hand in our papers, and the presiding pedagogue would give us marks, more or less, according to the accuracy with which 'our own words' had 'expressed' the meaning of the Bard.

He ought, of course, to have given us naught all round with a hundred lines to himself for ever having set us the silly exercise. Nobody's 'own words,' except those of Shakespeare himself, can possibly 'express' what Shakespeare meant. The substance of a work of art is inseparable from its form; its truth and its beauty are two and yet, mysteriously, one. The verbal expression of even a metaphysic or a system of ethics is very nearly as much of a work of art as a love poem. The philosophy of Plato expressed in the 'own words' of Jowett is not the philosophy of Plato; nor in the 'own words' of, say, Billy Sunday, is the teaching of St. Paul St. Paul's teaching.

'Our own words' are inadequate even to express the meaning of other words; how much more inadequate, when it is a matter of rendering meanings which have their original expression in terms of music or one of the visual arts! What, for example, does music 'say'? You can buy at almost any concert an analytical programme that will tell you exactly. Much too exactly; that is the trouble. Every analyst has his own version. Imagine Pharaoh's dream interpreted successively by Joseph, by the Egyptian soothsayers, by Freud, by Rivers, by Adler, by Jung, by Wohlgemuth: it would 'say' a great many different things. Not nearly so many, however, as the Fifth Symphony has been made to say in the verbiage of its analysts. Not nearly so many as the Virgin of the Rocks and the Sistine Madonna have no less lyrically said.

Annoyed by the verbiage and this absurd multiplicity

of attributed 'meanings,' some critics have protested that music and painting signify nothing but themselves; that the only things they 'say' are things, for example, about modulations and fugues, about colour values and three-dimensional forms. That they say anything about human destiny or the universe at large is a notion which these purists dismiss as merely nonsensical.

If the purists were right, then we should have to regard painters and musicians as monsters. For it is strictly impossible to be a human being and not to have views of some kind about the universe at large, very difficult to be a human being and not to express those views, at any rate by implication. Now, it is a matter of observation that painters and musicians are *not* monsters. Therefore . . . The conclusion follows, unescapably.

It is not only in programme music and problem pictures that composers and painters express their views about the universe. The purest and most abstract artistic creations can be, in their own peculiar language, as eloquent in this respect as the most deliberately tendencious.

Compare, for example, a Virgin by Piero della Francesca with a Virgin by Tura. Two Madonnas—and the current symbolical conventions are observed by both artists. The difference, the enormous difference between the two pictures is a purely pictorial difference, a difference in the forms and their arrangement, in the disposition of the lines and planes and masses. To any one in the least sensitive to the eloquence of pure form, the two Madonnas say utterly different things about the world.

Piero's composition is a welding together of smooth and beautifully balanced solidities. Everything in his universe is endowed with a kind of supernatural substantiality, is much more 'there' than any object of the actual world could possibly be. And how sublimely rational, in the noblest, the most humane acceptation of the word, how orderedly philosophical is the landscape, are all the inhabitants of this world! It is the creation of a god who 'ever plays the geometer.'

What does she say, this Madonna from San Sepolcro? If I have not wholly mistranslated the eloquence of Piero's forms, she is telling us of the greatness of the human spirit, of its power to rise above circumstance and dominate fate. If you were to ask her, 'How shall I be saved?' 'By Reason,' she would probably answer. And, anticipating Milton, 'Not only, not mainly upon the Cross,' she would say, 'is Paradise regained, but in those deserts of utter solitude where man puts forth the strength of his reason to resist the Fiend.' This particular mother of Christ is probably not a Christian.

Turn now to Tura's picture. It is fashioned out of a

substance that is like the living embodiment of flame—flame-flesh, alive and sensitive and suffering. His surfaces writhe away from the eye, as though shrinking, as though in pain. The lines flow intricately with something of that disquieting and, you feel, magical calligraphy, which characterizes certain Tibetan paintings. Look closely; feel your way into the picture, into the painter's thoughts and intuitions and emotions. This man was naked and at the mercy of destiny. To be able to proclaim the spirit's stoical independence, you must be able to raise your head above the flux of things; this man was sunk in it, overwhelmed. He could introduce no order into his world; it remained for him a mysterious chaos, fantastically marbled with patches, now of purest heaven, now of the most excruciating hell. A beautiful and terrifying world, is this Madonna's verdict; a world like the incarnation, the material projection, of Ophelia's madness. There are no certainties in it but suffering and occasional happiness. And as for salvation, who knows the way of salvation? There may perhaps be miracles, and there is always hope.

The limits of criticism are very quickly reached. When he has said 'in his own words' as much, or rather as little, as 'own words' can say, the critic can only refer his readers to the original work of art: let them go and see for themselves. Those who overstep the limit are either rather stupid, vain people, who love their 'own words' and imagine that they can say in them more than 'own words' are able in the nature of things to express. Or else they are intelligent people who happen to be philosophers or literary artists and who find it convenient to make the criticism of other men's work a jumping-off place for their own creativity.

What is true of painting is equally true of music. Music 'says' things about the world, but in specifically musical terms. Any attempt to reproduce these musical statements 'in our own words' is necessarily doomed to failure. We cannot isolate the truth contained in a piece of music; for it is a beauty-truth and inseparable from its partner. The best we can do is to indicate in the most general terms the nature of the musical beauty-truth under consideration and to refer curious truth-seekers to the original. Thus, the introduction to the *Benedictus* in the *Missa Solemnis* is a statement about the blessedness that is at the heart of things. But this is about as far as 'own words' will take us. If we were to start describing in our 'own words' exactly what Beethoven felt about this blessedness, how he conceived it, what he thought its nature to be, we should very soon find ourselves writing lyrical nonsense in the style of the analytical programme makers. Only music, and only Beethoven's music, and only this particular music of Beethoven, can tell us with any precision what Beethoven's conception of the blessedness at the heart of things actually was. If we want to know, we must listen—on a still June night, by preference, with the breathing of the invisible sea for background to the music and the scent of lime trees drifting through the darkness, like some exquisite soft harmony apprehended by another sense.

MEDITATION ON EL GRECO

THE pleasures of ignorance are as great, in their way, as the pleasures of knowledge. For though the light is good, though it is satisfying to be able to place the things that surround one in the categories of an ordered and comprehensible system, it is also good to find oneself sometimes in the dark, it is pleasant now and then to have to speculate with vague bewilderment about a world, which ignorance has reduced to a quantity of mutually irrelevant happenings dotted, like so many unexplored and fantastic islands, on the face of a vast ocean of incomprehension. For me, one of the greatest charms of travel consists in the fact that it offers unique opportunities for indulging in the luxury of ignorance. I am not one of those conscientious travellers who, before they visit a new country, spend weeks mugging up its geology, its economics, its art history, its literature.

I prefer, at any rate during my first few visits, to be a thoroughly unintelligent tourist. It is only later, when my ignorance has lost its virgin freshness, that I begin to read what the intelligent tourist would have known by heart before he bought his tickets. I read—and forthwith, in a series of apocalypses, my isolated and mysteriously odd impressions begin to assume significance, my jumbled memories fall harmoniously into patterns. The pleasures of ignorance have given place to the pleasures of knowledge.

I have only twice visited Spain—not often enough, that is to say, to have grown tired of ignorance. I still enjoy bewilderedly knowing as little as possible about all I see between the Pyrenees and Cape Trafalgar. Another two or three visits, and the time will be ripe for me to go to the London Library and look up 'Spain' in the subject index. In one of the numerous, the all too numerous, books there catalogued I shall find, no doubt, the explanation of a little mystery that has mildly and intermittently puzzled me for quite a number of years—ever since, at one of those admirable Loan Exhibitions in Burlington House, I saw for the first time a version of El Greco's *Dream of Philip II*.

This curious composition, familiar to every visitor to the Escorial, represents the king, dressed and gloved like an undertaker in inky black, kneeling on a well-

MEDITATION ON EL GRECO

stuffed cushion in the centre foreground; beyond him, on the left, a crowd of pious kneelers, some lay, some clerical, but all manifestly saintly, are looking upwards into a heaven full of waltzing angels, cardinal virtues and biblical personages, grouped in a circle round the Cross and the luminous monogram of the Saviour. On the right a very large whale gigantically yawns, and a vast concourse, presumably of the damned, is hurrying (in spite of all that we learned in childhood about the anatomy of whales) down its crimson throat. A curious picture, I repeat, and, as a work of art, not remarkably good; there are many much better Grecos belonging even to the same youthful period. Nevertheless, in spite of its mediocrity, it is a picture for which I have a special weakness. I like it for the now sadly unorthodox reason that the subject interests me. And the subject interests me, because I do not know what the subject is. For this dream of King Philip—what was it? Was it a visionary anticipation of the Last Judgment? A mystical peep into Heaven? An encouraging glimpse of the Almighty's short way with heretics? I do not know—do not at present even desire to know. In the face of so extravagant a phantasy as this of Greco's, the pleasures of ignorance are peculiarly intense. Confronted by the mysterious whale, the undertaker king, the swarming aërial saints and scurrying sinners, I give my fancy licence and fairly wallow in the pleasure of bewilderedly not knowing.

The fancy I like best of all that have occurred to me is the one which affirms that this queer picture was painted as a prophetic and symbolic autobiography, that it was meant to summarize hieroglyphically the whole of Greco's future development. For that whale in the right foreground—that great-grandfather of Moby Dick, with his huge yawn, his crimson gullet and the crowd of the damned descending, like bank clerks at six o'clock into the Underground—that whale, I say, is the most significantly autobiographical object in all El Greco's early pictures. For whither are they bound, those hastening damned? 'Down the red lane,' as our nurses used to say when they were encouraging us to swallow the uneatable viands of childhood. Down the red lane into a dim inferno of tripes. Down, in a word, into that strange and rather frightful universe which Greco's spirit seems to have come more and more exclusively, as he grew older, to inhabit. For in the Cretan's later painting every personage is a Jonah. Yes, *every* personage. Which is where *The Dream of Philip II* reveals itself as being imperfectly prophetic, a mutilated symbol. It is for the damned alone that the whale opens his mouth. If El Greco had wanted to tell the whole truth about his future development, he would have sent the blessed to join them, or at least have provided his saints and angels with another monster of their own, a supernal whale floating head downwards among the clouds, with a second red lane ascending, strait and narrow, towards a swallowed Heaven. Paradise and Purgatory, Hell, and even the common Earth—for El Greco in his artistic maturity, every department of the universe was situated in the belly of a whale. His Annunciations and Assumptions, his Agonies and Transfigurations and Crucifixions, his Martyrdoms and Stigmatizations are all, without exception, visceral events. Heaven is no larger than the Black Hole of Calcutta, and God Himself is whale-engulfed.

Critics have tried to explain El Greco's pictorial agorophobia in terms of his early, Cretan education. There is no space in his pictures, they assure us, because the typical art of that Byzantium, which was El Greco's spiritual home, was the mosaic, and the mosaic is innocent of depth. A specious explanation, whose only defect is that it happens to be almost entirely beside the point. To begin with, the Byzantine mosaic was not invariably without depth. Those extraordinary eighth-century mosaics in the Omeyyid mosque at Damascus, for example, are as spacious and airy as impressionist landscapes. They are, it is true, somewhat exceptional specimens of the art. But even the commoner shut-in mosaics have really nothing to do with El Greco's painting, for the Byzantine saints and kings are enclosed, or, to be more accurate, are flatly inlaid in a kind of two-dimensional abstraction—in a pure Euclidean, plane-geometrical Heaven of gold or blue. Their universe never bears the smallest resemblance to that whale's belly in which every one of El Greco's personages has his or her mysterious and appalling being. El Greco's world is no Flatland; there is depth in it—just a little depth. It is precisely this that makes it seem such a disquieting world. In their two-dimensional abstraction the personages of the Byzantine mosaists are perfectly at home; they are adapted to their environment. But, solid and three-dimensional, made to be the inhabitants of a spacious universe, El Greco's people are shut up in a world where there is perhaps just room enough to swing a cat, but no more. They are in prison and, which makes it worse, in a visceral prison. For all that surrounds them is organic, animal. Clouds, rock, drapery have all been mysteriously transformed into mucus and skinned muscle and peritoneum. The Heaven into which Count Orgaz ascends is like some cosmic operation for appendicitis. The Madrid *Resurrection* is a resurrection in a digestive tube. And from the later pictures we receive the gruesome impression that all the personages, both human and divine, have begun to suffer a

MEDITATION ON EL GRECO

process of digestion, are being gradually assimilated to their visceral surroundings. Even in the Madrid *Resurrection* the forms and texture of the naked flesh have assumed a strangely tripe-like aspect. In the case of the nudes in *Laocoon* and *The Opening of the Seventh Seal* (both of them works of El Greco's last years) this process of assimilation has been carried a good deal further. After seeing their draperies and the surrounding landscape gradually peptonized and transformed, the unhappy Jonahs of Toledo discover, to their horror, that they themselves are being digested. Their bodies, their arms and legs, their faces, fingers, toes are ceasing to be humanly their own; they are becoming—the process is slow but inexorably sure—part of the universal Whale's internal workings. It is lucky for them that El Greco died when he did. Twenty years more, and the Trinity, the Communion of Saints and all the human race would have found themselves reduced to hardly distinguishable excrescences on the surface of a cosmic gut. The most favoured might perhaps have aspired to be taenias and trematodes.

For myself, I am very sorry that El Greco did not live to be as old as Titian. At eighty or ninety he would have been producing an almost abstract art—a cubism without cubes, organic, purely visceral. What pictures he would then have painted! Beautiful, thrilling, profoundly appalling. For appalling are even the pictures he painted in middle age, dreadful in spite of their extraordinary power and beauty. This swallowed universe into which he introduces us is one of the most disquieting creations of the human mind. One of the most puzzling too. For what were El Greco's reasons for driving mankind down the red lane? What induced him to take God out of His boundless Heaven and shut Him up in a fish's gut? One can only obscurely speculate. All that I am quite certain of is that there were profounder and more important reasons for the whale than the memory of the mosaics—the wholly unvisceral mosaics—which he may have seen in the course of a Cretan childhood, a Venetian and Roman youth. Nor will a disease of the eye account, as some have claimed, for his strange artistic development. Diseases must be very grave indeed before they become completely coextensive with their victims. That men are affected by their illnesses is obvious; but it is no less obvious that, except when they are almost *in extremis,* they are something more than the sum of their morbid symptoms. Dostoevsky was not merely personified epilepsy, Keats was other things besides a simple lump of pulmonary tuberculosis. Men make use of their illnesses at least as much as they are made use of by them. It is likely enough that El Greco had something wrong with his eyes. But other people have had the same disease without for that reason painting pictures like the *Laocoon* and *The Opening of the Seventh Seal*. To say that El Greco was just a defective eyesight is absurd; he was a man who used a defective eyesight.

Used it for what purpose? to express what strange feeling about the world, what mysterious philosophy? It is hard indeed to answer. For El Greco belongs as a metaphysician (every significant artist is a metaphysician, a propounder of beauty-truths and form-theories) to no known school. The most one can say, by way of classification, is that, like most of the great artists of the Baroque, he believed in the validity of ecstasy, of the non-rational, 'numinous' experiences out of which, as a raw material, the reason fashions the gods or the various attributes of God. But the kind of ecstatic experience artistically rendered and meditated on by El Greco was quite different from the kind of experience which is described and symbolically 'rationalized' in the painting, sculpture and architecture of the great Baroque artists of the *seicento*. Those mass-producers of spirituality, the Jesuits, had perfected a simple technique for the fabrication of orthodox ecstasies. They had cheapened an experience, hitherto accessible only to the spiritually wealthy, and so placed it within the reach of all. What the Italian *seicento* artists so brilliantly and copiously rendered was this cheapened experience and the metaphysic in terms of which it could be rationalized. 'St. Teresa for All.' 'A John of the Cross in every Home.' Such were, or might have been, their slogans. Was it to be wondered at if their sublimities were a trifle theatrical, their tendernesses treacly, their spiritual intuitions rather commonplace and vulgar? Even the greatest of the Baroque artists were not remarkable for subtlety and spiritual refinement.

With these rather facile ecstasies and the orthodox Counter-Reformation theology in terms of which they could be interpreted, El Greco has nothing to do. The bright reassuring Heaven, the smiling or lachrymose, but always all too human divinities, the stage immensities and stage mysteries, all the stock-in-trade of the *seicentisti*, are absent from his pictures. There is ecstasy and flamy aspiration; but always ecstasy and aspiration, as we have seen, within the belly of a whale. El Greco seems to be talking all the time about the physiological root of ecstasy, not the spiritual flower; about the primary corporeal facts of numinous experience, not the mental derivatives from them. However vulgarly, the artists of the Baroque were concerned with the flower, not the root, with the derivatives and theological interpretations, not the brute facts of immediate physical experience. Not that they were ignorant of the physio-

MEDITATION ON EL GRECO

logical nature of these primary facts. Bernini's astonishing *St. Teresa* proclaims it in the most unequivocal fashion; and it is interesting to note that in this statue (as well as in the very similar and equally astonishing *Ludovica Albertoni* in San Francesco a Ripa) he gives to the draperies a kind of organic and, I might say, intestinal lusciousness of form. A little softened, smoothed and simplified, the robe of the great mystic would be indistinguishable from the rest of the swallowed landscape inside El Greco's whale. Bernini saves the situation (from the Counter-Reformer's point of view) by introducing into his composition the figure of the dart-brandishing angel. This aerial young creature is the inhabitant of an unswallowed Heaven. He carries with him the implication of infinite spaces. Charmingly and a little preposterously (the hand which holds the fiery dart has a delicately crook'd little finger, like the hand of some too refined young person in the act of raising her tea-cup), the angel symbolizes the spiritual flower of ecstasy, whose physiological root is the swooning Teresa in her peritoneal robe. Bernini is, spiritually speaking, a *plein-airiste*.

Not so El Greco. So far as he is concerned, there is nothing outside the whale. The primary physiological fact of religious experience is also, for him, the final fact. He remains consistently on the plane of that visceral consciousness which we so largely ignore, but with which our ancestors (as their language proves) did so much of their feeling and thinking. 'Where is thy zeal and thy strength, the sounding of the bowels and of thy mercies towards me?' 'My heart is turned within me, my repentings are kindled together.' 'I will bless the Lord who hath given me counsel; my reins also instruct me in the night season.' 'For God is my record, how greatly I long after you all in the bowels of Jesus Christ.' 'For Thou hast possessed my reins.' 'Is Ephraim my dear son? . . . Therefore my bowels are troubled for him.' The Bible abounds in such phrases—phrases which strike the modern reader as queer, a bit indelicate, even repellent. We are accustomed to thinking of ourselves as thinking entirely with our heads. Wrongly, as the physiologists have shown. For what we think and feel and are is to a great extent determined by the state of our ductless glands and our viscera. The Psalmist drawing instruction from his reins, the Apostle with his yearning bowels, are thoroughly in the modern physiological movement.

El Greco lived at a time when the reality of the primary visceral consciousness was still recognized—when the heart and the liver, the spleen and reins did all a man's feeling for him, and the four humours of blood, phlegm, choler and melancholy determined his character and imposed his passing moods. Even the loftiest experiences were admitted to be primarily physiological. Teresa knew God in terms of an exquisite pain in her heart, her side, her bowels. But while Teresa, and along with her the generality of human beings, found it natural to pass from the realm of physiology into that of the spirit—from the belly of the whale out into the wide open sky—El Greco obstinately insisted on remaining swallowed. His meditations were all of religious experience and ecstasy—but always of religious experience in its raw physiological state, always of primary, immediate, visceral ecstasy. He expressed these meditations in terms of Christian symbols—of symbols, that is to say, habitually employed to describe experiences quite different from the primary physiological states on which he was accustomed to dwell. It is the contrast between these symbols, with their currently accepted significance, and the special private use to which El Greco puts them—it is this strange contrast which gives to El Greco's pictures their peculiarly disquieting quality. For the Christian symbols remind us of all the spiritual open spaces—the open spaces of altruistic feeling, the open spaces of abstract thought, the open spaces of free-floating spiritual ecstasy. El Greco imprisons them, claps them up in a fish's gut. The symbols of the spiritual open spaces are compelled by him to serve as a language in terms of which he talks about the close immediacies of visceral awareness, about the ecstasy that annihilates the personal soul, not by dissolving it out into universal infinity, but by drawing it down and drowning it in the warm, pulsating, tremulous darkness of the body.

Well, I have wandered far and fancifully from the undertaker king and his enigmatic nightmare of whales and Jonahs. But imaginative wandering is the privilege of the ignorant. When one doesn't know one is free to invent. I have seized the opportunity while it presented itself. One of these days I may discover what the picture is about, and when that has happened I shall no longer be at liberty to impose my own interpretations. Imaginative criticism is essentially an art of ignorance. It is only because we don't know what a writer or artist meant to say that we are free to concoct meanings of our own. If El Greco had somewhere specifically told us what he meant to convey by painting in terms of Black Holes and mucus, I should not now be in a position to speculate. But luckily he never told us; I am justified in letting my fancy loose to wander.

SECTION II

MEDITATION
IN ARUNDEL STREET

A WALK down Arundel Street in London remains, after all, the best introduction to philosophy. Keep your eyes to the left as you descend towards the river from the Strand. You will observe that the *Christian World* is published at number seven, and a few yards further down, at number nine, the *Feathered World*. By the time you have reached the Embankment you will find yourself involved in the most abstruse metaphysical speculations.

The Christian World, the Feathered World—between them a great gulf is fixed, a gulf which only St. Francis has ever tried to bridge, and with singularly little success. His sermon to the birds was ineffective. In spite of it, the gulf still yawns. No Christians have grown feathers and no feathered people are Christians. The values and even the truths current in the world of number seven Arundel Street cease to hold good in that of number nine.

The world of the Christians and the world of the feathered are but two out of a swarm of humanly conceivable and humanly explorable worlds. They constellate the thinking mind like stars, and between them stretches the mental equivalent of interstellar space—unspanned. Between, for example, a human body and the whizzing electrons of which it is composed, and the thoughts, the feelings which direct its movements, there are, as yet at any rate, no visible connections. The gulf that separates the lover's, say, or the musician's world from the world of the chemist is deeper, more uncompromisingly unbridgeable than that which divides Anglo-Catholics from macaws or geese from Primitive Methodists. We cannot walk from one of these worlds into another; we can only jump. The last act of *Don Giovanni* is not deducible from electrons, or molecules, or even from cells and entire organs. In relation to these physical, chemical, and biological worlds it is simply a *non sequitur*. The whole of our universe is composed of a series of such *non sequiturs*. The only reason for supposing that there is in fact any connection between the logically and scientifically unrelated fragments of our experience is simply the fact that the experience is *ours*, that we have the fragments in our consciousness. These constellated worlds are all situated in the heaven of the human mind. Some day, conceivably, the scientific and logical engineers may build us convenient bridges from one world to another. Meanwhile we must be content to hop. *Solvitur saltando.* The only walking you can do in Arundel Street is along the pavements.

MEDITATION ON THE MOON

MATERIALISM and mentalism—the philosophies of 'nothing but.' How wearily familiar we have become with that 'nothing but space, time, matter and motion,' that 'nothing but sex,' that 'nothing but economics'! And the no less intolerant 'nothing but spirit,' 'nothing but consciousness,' 'nothing but psychology'—how boring and tiresome they also are! 'Nothing but' is mean as well as stupid. It lacks generosity. Enough of 'nothing but.' It is time to say again, with primitive common sense (but for better reasons), 'not only, but also.'

Outside my window the night is struggling to wake; in the moonlight, the blinded garden dreams so vividly of its lost colours that the black roses are almost crimson, the trees stand expectantly on the verge of living greenness. The white-washed parapet of the terrace is brilliant against the dark-blue sky. (Does the oasis lie there below, and, beyond the last of the palm trees, is that the desert?) The white walls of the house coldly reverberate the lunar radiance. (Shall I turn to look at the Dolomites rising naked out of the long slopes of snow?) The moon is full. And not only full, but also beautiful. And not only beautiful, but also . . .

Socrates was accused by his enemies of having affirmed, heretically, that the moon was a stone. He denied the accusation. All men, said he, know that the moon is a god, and he agreed with all men. As an answer to the materialistic philosophy of 'nothing but' his retort was sensible and even scientific. More sensible and scientific, for instance, than the retort invented by D. H. Lawrence in that strange book, so true in its psychological substance, so preposterous, very often, in its pseudo-scientific form, *Fantasia of the Unconscious*. 'The moon,' writes Lawrence, 'certainly isn't a snowy cold world, like a world of our own gone cold. Nonsense. It is a globe of dynamic substance, like radium or phosphorus, coagulated upon a vivid pole of energy.' The defect of this statement is that it happens to be demonstrably untrue. The moon is quite certainly not made of radium or phosphorus. The moon is, materially, a 'stone.' Lawrence was angry (and he did well to be angry) with the nothing-but philosophers who insist that the moon is only a stone. He knew that it was something more; he had the empirical certainty of its deep significance and importance. But he tried to explain this empirically established fact of its significance in the wrong terms—in terms of matter and not of spirit. To say that the moon is made of radium is nonsense. But to say, with Socrates, that it is made of god-stuff is strictly accurate. For there is nothing, of course, to prevent the moon from being both a stone and a god. The evidence for its stoniness and against its radiuminess may be found in any children's encyclopaedia. It carries an absolute conviction. No less convincing, however, is the evidence for the moon's divinity. It may be extracted from our own experiences, from the writings of the poets, and, in fragments, even from certain textbooks of physiology and medicine.

But what is this 'divinity'? How shall we define a 'god'? Expressed in psychological terms (which are primary—there is no getting behind them), a god is something that gives us the peculiar kind of feeling which Professor Otto has called 'numinous' (from the Latin *numen*, a supernatural being). Numinous feelings are the original god-stuff, from which the theory-making mind extracts the individualized gods of the pantheons, the various attributes of the One. Once formulated, a theology evokes in its turn numinous feelings. Thus, men's terrors in face of the enigmatically dangerous universe led them to postulate the existence of angry gods; and, later, thinking about angry gods made them feel terror, even when the universe was giving them, for the moment, no cause of alarm. Emotion, rationalization, emotion—the process is circular and continuous. Man's religious life works on the principle of a hot-water system.

The moon is a stone; but it is a highly numinous stone. Or, to be more precise, it is a stone about which and because of which men and women have numinous feelings. Thus, there is a soft moonlight that can give us the peace that passes understanding. There is a moonlight that inspires a kind of awe. There is a cold and austere moonlight that tells the soul of its loneliness and desperate isolation, its insignificance or its uncleanness. There is an amorous moonlight prompting to love—to love not only for an individual but sometimes even for the whole universe. But the moon shines on the body as well as, through the windows of the eyes, within the mind. It affects the soul directly; but it can affect it also by obscure and circuitous ways—through the blood. Half the human race lives in manifest obedience to the lunar rhythm; and there is evidence to show that the physiological and therefore the spiritual life, not only of women, but of men too, mysteriously ebbs and flows with the changes of the moon. There are unreasoned joys, inexplicable miseries, laughters and remorses without a cause. Their sudden and fantastic alternations constitute the ordinary weather of our minds. These moods, of which the more gravely numinous may be hypostasized as gods, the lighter, if we will, as hobgoblins and fairies, are the children of the blood and humours. But the blood and humours obey, among many other masters, the changing moon. Touching the soul directly through the eyes and, indirectly, along the dark channels of the blood, the moon is doubly a divinity. Even dogs and wolves, to judge at least by their nocturnal howlings, seem to feel in some dim bestial fashion a kind of numinous emotion about the full moon. Artemis, the goddess of wild things, is identified in the later mythology with Selene.

Even if we think of the moon as only a stone, we shall find its very stoniness potentially a *numen*. A stone gone cold. An airless, waterless stone and the prophetic image of our own earth when, some few million years from now, the senescent sun shall have lost its present fostering power. . . . And so on. This passage could easily be prolonged—a Study in Purple. But I forbear. Let every reader lay on as much of the royal rhetorical colour as he finds to his taste. Anyhow, purple or no purple, there the stone is—stony. You cannot think about it for long without finding yourself invaded by one or other of several essentially numinous sentiments. These sentiments belong to one or other of two contrasted and complementary groups. The name of the first family is Sentiments of Human Insignificance, of the second, Sentiments of Human Greatness. Meditating on that derelict stone afloat there in the abyss, you may feel most numinously a worm, abject and futile in the face of wholly incomprehensible immensities. 'The silence of those infinite spaces frightens me.' You may feel as Pascal felt. Or, alternatively, you may feel as M. Paul Valéry has said that he feels. 'The silence of those infinite spaces does *not* frighten me.' For the spectacle of that stony astronomical moon need not necessarily make you feel like a worm. It may, on the contrary, cause you to rejoice exultantly in your manhood. There floats the stone, the nearest and most familiar symbol of all the astronomical horrors; but the astronomers who discovered those horrors of space and time were men. The universe throws down a challenge to the human spirit; in spite of his insignificance and abjection, man has taken it up. The stone glares down at us out of the black boundlessness, a *memento mori*. But the fact that we know it for a *memento mori* justifies us in feeling a certain human pride. We have a right to our moods of sober exultation.

ON GRACE

'MERIT,' writes Michelet in the course of an attack on the Christian conception of Grace, 'merit is said to consist in being loved, in being the elect of God, predestined to salvation. And demerit, damnation? Being hated by God, condemned in advance, created for damnation.' This was more than a passionately convinced democrat could swallow. 'Who can believe nowadays that God saves according to favour, that salvation is an arbitrary and capricious privilege? Whatever any one may say, the world to-day believes, and believes with unshaken faith, in justice, equal justice, without privileges.' Charles Péguy, in one of his youthful writings, developed the same theme. For 'just as we are one (solidaires) with the damned of the earth . . . even so . . . we are one with the eternal damned. We do not admit that there should be human beings treated inhumanly; that there should be citizens treated uncivically or men thrust out from the gate of any city. Here is the deep movement by which we are animated, the great movement of universality which animates the Kantian ethic and which animates us in our claims. We do not admit that there should be a single exception, that any door should be shut in any one's face. Heaven or earth, we do not admit that there should be fragments of the city not living within the city.'

'No more elect.' The words are an admirable war-cry. But a war-cry is seldom, perhaps never, a truth. 'No more elect' is the expression of a wish, not the statement of a fact. For are there not, in the very nature of things, certain doors which, for some people, must always remain closed, certain unescapable and foredoomed damnations, certain inevitable elections? Pelagians and Arminians, Humanitarians and Democrats (under the different names, the heresy remains the same) have answered: No. It is always in man's power to shape his own ends; human effort, right action are always enough. But not only orthodoxy, the facts themselves, it seems to me, condemn such heretics. For here and now, and quite apart from any hypothetical after-life, are not Grace and Reprobation observable facts? Unpleasant facts, no doubt—but so, sometimes, is gravitation, a very unpleasant fact indeed when, at the top of a skyscraper, your elevator cable breaks. No amount of disbelief, no amount of not admitting will prevent people who have stepped over the edges of precipices from falling to the bottom. To put fences round quarries is right and reasonable; to pretend that it is impossible to fall is silly. Michelet and Péguy, it seems to me, are like men who refuse to admit the existence of gravitation. 'To every one that hath shall be given and from him that hath not shall be taken away even that which he hath,' is the formulation of a natural law. We can do something to limit the operation of this law, just as we can do something (by means of fences, parachutes, and what not) to limit the operation of the law of gravitation. For example, certain social gulfs can be fenced round with legislation. We can make it possible for one man not to have political powers that are not shared by his fellows. We can abolish the extremes of wealth and poverty. We can give all children the same education. The operation of the law of Grace will, by these means, be limited; but we can no more abolish the law itself than we can abolish the law of gravitation. Occasions for the law to manifest itself—these are all we can abolish, and not a very great number even of those. For though we can prevent one man from having more money than another, we cannot equalize their congenital wealth of wits and charm, of sensitiveness and strength of will, of beauty, courage, special talents. To those who, quite unjustly, have much of this hereditary wealth, much in the form of valuable personal experience, of knowledge, power, and social influence will be given; from those who lack it, the little they have will be taken away. Democrats do their best to prevent any doors being slammed in the faces of the not-having, or specially opened for the elect; but in vain. For though we can prevent one man from possessing political, economic, or educational privileges not shared by his fellows, we cannot prevent him (if he is naturally gifted) from making incomparably better use of his educational privileges than they do, from spending his money in a more human and comely manner, and from wielding power over those who do not like responsibility and whose only desire is to be led. The man who said '*Plus d'élus*,' was himself one of the elect—at any rate in certain respects. For a man may have (and will be suitably rewarded for the having) a certain kind of spiritual wealth and at the same time lack (and be punished for the lacking) certain other gifts and graces. Intellectually, for example, he may have and it will be given him; but emotionally and aesthetically, it may be taken away from him because he has not.

Humanly speaking, the Nature of Things is profoundly inequitable. It is impossible to justify the ways of God to man in terms of human morality or even of human reason. In the final chapters of the Book of Job God is justified, not by His goodness, not by the reasonableness of what He ordains, but because, as His strange, enigmatic, and often sinister creations attest, He is powerful and dangerous and gloriously inventive beyond all human conception; because He is at once so appalling and so admirable, that we cannot sufficiently love or fear Him, because, in the last resort, He is absolutely incomprehensible. The wild ass and the untamable unicorn, the war-horse laughing among the trumpets, the hawk and the fierce eagle, 'whose young ones also suck up blood'—these are God's emblems, these the heraldic beasts emblazoned on the banners of Heaven. The arguments uttered from the whirlwind—or rather the mere statements of prodigious fact—are too much for Job. He admits that he has been talking about things 'I understand not, things too wonderful for me which I know not.' 'Wherefore I abhor myself and repent in dust and ashes.' Job's, it seems to me, is the final word on this disquieting subject. In Ivan Karamazov's phrase, we must 'accept the universe' not merely in spite of the frightful and incomprehensible things which go on in it, but actually, to some extent, because of them. We must accept it, among other reasons, because it is, from our human point of view,

ON GRACE

entirely and divinely unacceptable. 'Wilt thou condemn me that thou mayst be righteous?' God asks, and, without deigning to explain what His own righteousness may be, He proceeds to round off His extraordinary zoological argument with Behemoth and Leviathan. 'The one,' God explains, 'moveth his tail like a cedar, the sinews of his stones are wrapped together.' As for the other, 'who can open the doors of his face? his teeth are terrible round about.' Behemoth and Leviathan are more convincing than the most flawless syllogisms. Job is overwhelmed, flattened out; the divine logic moves on the feet of elephants.

'Merit consists in being loved, elected by God, predestined to salvation.' And 'justice is not enough.' Michelet was angry with the Christians for making these assertions. But at bottom, and when freed from their mythological incrustations, these assertions happen unfortunately to be true. Our universe is the universe of Behemoth and Leviathan, not of Helvetius and Godwin. Salvation in this Behemoth-world (to say nothing of success) is not the necessary reward of what we regard as merit; it is the fruit of certain inborn qualities of spirit (qualities which may be humanly meritorious—or may not); in other words, it is the result of favouritism and predestination. Justice is not enough; faith (in the sense of something non-moral, but somehow God-pleasing) is also necessary—indeed, in some cases is alone sufficient to guarantee salvation. Personal integrity, happiness, even the general good can be achieved by, humanly speaking, immoral people and as the result of committing unjust acts; whereas the just acts of moral but unfortunately predestined, God-displeasing people can result in damnation for the meritorious actors and disasters for those around them. In that strange and very beautiful book, *The Castle*, Franz Kafka has written, in terms of a nightmarishly realistic allegory, of the incommensurability between divine values and human values. Judged by human standards, the officials in his heavenly Castle are malignantly capricious and inefficient almost to the point of imbecility. When they reward it is by mere favouritism, and when they punish it is as often as not for honourable and rational acts. Above all, they are never consistent. For sometimes the moral and reasonable people find themselves rewarded (for it so happens that they are somehow God-pleasing as well as moral and reasonable); and sometimes the immoral and unreasonable ones find themselves (as we think they should be) severely punished—but punished for actions which, in others, more happily predestined, were counted as a merit. There is no knowing. And that there should be no knowing is precisely the 'point' of the Nature of Things.

In that unknowableness consists a part at least of its divinity, and one of our reasons for accepting the universe is just this fact: that it propounds to us an insoluble riddle.

Here I must draw a very necessary distinction between salvation and success. (I use this last word, not in its restricted Smilesian sense, but in its widest possible significance. Cézanne never sold any of his pictures; but he was a highly successful painter, successful, that is to say, in relation to painting.) Those who have talents will be rewarded for their good fortune with appropriate success; but it does not follow that they will be given salvation—salvation, I mean, in the present; for we cannot profitably discuss the hypothetical future after death. There may or may not be a posthumous Kingdom of Heaven; but there is certainly, as Jesus insisted, a Kingdom of Heaven within us, accessible during life. Salvation in this inward heaven is a certain sentiment of personal integrity and fulfilment, a profoundly satisfying consciousness of being 'in order.' (*In sua volontà e nostra pace.*) For normal men and women a consciousness of having behaved in a, humanly speaking, meritorious fashion is, in many cases, a necessary pre-requisite to this salvation. But by no means in all cases. One can feel fulfilled and in order for no better reason than that the morning happens to be fine. Salvation is a state of mind, is what we have in our consciousness, when the various elements of our being are in harmony among themselves, and with the world which surrounds us. To achieve this harmony, we may have to behave meritoriously—but equally we may not have to do anything of the kind. It is possible for us to be harmonized gratuitously—in orthodox language, to be saved by God's grace.

The greater and the more exceptional are a man's success-earning gifts, the harder, as a rule, will it be for him to achieve that harmony of which the consciousness is salvation. The poor in spirit are less successful than the rich in spirit, but they are for that very reason more liable to be saved. Thanks to their poverty, they are actually unaware of many of the possibilities of discord which it is so easy for the richly gifted to turn into actual disharmony. True, the salvation of the rich in spirit, when they do achieve harmony, is a better salvation than that of the poor in spirit; heaven has its spheres. But harmony is always harmony, and, on their lower plane, the poor in spirit are as genuinely saved as the rich on theirs. Also more of them are saved, both absolutely and in proportion to their total numbers. Cosmic injustice is thus seen to be tempered by a certain compensatory kindness to the dispossessed, who turn out after all to be the possessors of something which entitles them to receive a gift. This something (which, so far as success is concerned, is nothing, has a negative value) is their poverty. The law of Grace holds good even here: 'for unto every one that hath shall be given.' The poor have poverty and are given salvation; they have no talents, and success is therefore taken away from them. Those, on the contrary, who have talents are given success; but having no easily harmonizable simplicity, they are not given salvation, or given it only grudgingly. It is almost as difficult for the spiritually rich to enter the kingdom of heaven as it is for the materially rich.

Success is given to those who have talents; but in many cases it is given only when the talents are used in a, humanly speaking, meritorious way. There are also many cases in which the consciousness of having acted meritoriously is necessary to personal salvation. But to help to individual success or individual salvation is only a secondary and incidental function of morality. The essential 'point' of meritorious behaviour is that it is socially valuable behaviour. The individual succeeds because of his talents and is saved by grace—because he has certain saving peculiarities of character or has performed some usually non-moral but God-pleasing act of 'faith.' Works are the things which save, not the individual, but society, which mitigate the injustices of a world, of which Behemoth is the emblem. Putting fences round quarries—that is works.

Christianity approves of putting fences round quarries; but it also insists very strongly on the fact that the quarries exist and that the law of gravitation is unalterable. In this it shows itself to be thoroughly scientific; though it is doubtless not quite so scientific in identifying one of the non-moral conditions of salvation with belief in the Athanasian Creed. Democratic humanitarianism is not scientific. Its apostles proclaim salvation by works and seem to believe that the law of Grace, if it exists, can be repealed by Act of Parliament. Not content with putting fences round quarries, such humanitarians as Michelet and Péguy paradoxically deny the possibility of falling. If people in fact do fall, that is due to the malignity of certain of their fellows, not to the operation of a natural law.

If the world is a bad place (and Behemoth is not remarkable for his virtues), ought religious myths to be true? To admit the existence of the bad facts, to incorporate them in a religious myth is, in a sense, to condone and even sanctify them. But evil should not be condoned or sanctified; to change what we regard as bad is the first of human duties. In the fight against evil, are not all weapons legitimate? One cannot disparage a thing more effectively than by saying that it does not exist, or that if it does exist, its being is only accidental and temporary. Purely practical religions, like Christian Science and democratic humanitarianism, make free use of these weapons of ostrich-like denial and deliberate ignorance. Seeking to cure the sick, the Christian Scientists refuse to admit that there is really such a thing as sickness. Attacking injustice, the humanitarians deny the existence of Grace. From the advertising agent's point of view they are probably right. *'No more Sickness'* and *'Plus d'élus'* are admirable slogans, guaranteed to sell large consignments of Christian Science and democratic humanitarianism in a remarkably short space of time. But will they go on selling the goods? And even now do they sell them to everybody? The answer to the second question is: No, there are many people to whom these slogans do not appeal. And presumably there will be such people in the future; so that the answer to the first question is only a tempered affirmative. *'No more Sickness'* and *'Plus d'élus'* will go on selling the goods to some people, never to all. To be accepted by most people over long periods, myths must be at bottom true as well as useful. The successful religions are at any rate partially scientific; they accept the universe, including evil, including Behemoth, including the rank injustice of Grace.

A danger besets the scientific, the too realistic religions: they may find themselves proclaiming that whatever is, is right. Facts are not necessarily good for being facts; it is easy, however, to believe so. The human mind has a tendency to attribute, not only existence to what it considers valuable, but also value to what is.

If we accept the universe, we must accept it for purely Jobic reasons—for its divinely appalling and divinely beautiful inhumanity, or, in other words, because, by our standards, it is utterly unacceptable. We must accept Behemoth, but accept him, among other reasons, that we may the better fight with him.

Grace is a fact, and the law of Grace ineluctable. But a religious myth which took account only of Grace and omitted to speak of Justice would be very unsatisfactory. Nietzsche's is such a myth. The values he transvaluates are the social values, and he transvaluates them into the values of Grace. '*Rien que les élus*,' says the philosopher of Grace: nothing but the elect, and those who are not the elect are nothing. The law of Grace should be allowed to operate without restriction. No fences round any quarry; those whom Nature has reprobated should be encouraged to fall. Such a doctrine is all very well for chronically moribund men of genius living quite alone in Alpine hotels or boarding-houses on the Riviera. (I myself always feel intensely aristocratic after a month or two of isolation in the Dolomites or by the Tyrrhenian.) But for the people who, in prosaic London or Berlin or Paris, have to do the actual pushing over precipices, for the people who have to be pushed . . . ? One has only to put the question to realize that a religion of unmitigated Grace simply won't do.

As usual, we must split the difference; or rather, we must preserve the difference and simply lay the two incompatibles together, Grace and Justice, side by side, without making any vain attempt to reconcile their contradiction. Mutually hostile, these two principles of Grace and Justice can be reconciled in practice by those who feel what is called, in the jargon of democratic theology, 'the sentiment of solidarity'—by those, in other words, who love their fellows. Some men and women have a special talent for love; they are as few, I think, as those who have a special talent for painting or mathematics. To the congenitally less gifted, Christianity and, more recently, Humanitarianism have tried to teach the art of loving. It is an art very difficult to acquire, and the successes of its Christian and democratic teachers have not been considerable. Most people do not love their fellows, or love them only in the abstract and when they aren't there. In moments of crisis, it is true, they may be carried away by the 'sentiment of solidarity,' they may feel one with *'les damnés de la terre, les forçats de la faim.*' But disasters are not chronic, and at ordinary times the feelings of most of us towards the damned of the earth are practically non-existent. Unless their case is brought violently to our notice, we simply don't think about them. In time, perhaps, as the science of psychology becomes more adequate, a better technique of teaching men how to love one another may be discovered. (Alternatively, of course, our descendants may develop a new social order, something like that of Mr. Wells's Selenites—an insect society in which love is perfectly unnecessary.) Scientific psychology may succeed where Christianity and the political religions have failed. Let us hope so. In a world where most people had been taught to love their fellows there would be no difficulty in reconciling the claims of Grace with those of Justice, of universality with favouritism. But in this actual world, where so few people love their neighbours, where those who have not envy those who have and where those who have despise or, more often, simply ignore, simply are unaware of, those who have not—in this actual world of ours the reconcilement is difficult indeed.

SQUEAK AND GIBBER

In the most high and palmy state of Rome,
A little ere the mightiest Julius fell,
The graves stood tenantless, and the sheeted dead
Did squeak and gibber in the Roman streets.

POETICALLY, of course, they could have done nothing else but squeak and gibber. They could never, for example, have cried and muttered, nor wailed and whispered, still less have indulged in hauntings and direct voice manifestations. The mysterious laws of poetry demanded that they should squeak and gibber and do nothing but squeak and gibber. Squeaking and gibbering are, in the circumstances, artistically inevitable; they are also, as it happens, historically correct. For the Roman dead, at any rate in the earlier, higher, and palmier phases of Roman history, *did* squeak and gibber. They squeaked as feebly and they gibbered as ineffectively as those poor anaemic ghosts for whom Odysseus prepared, on the border of Hades, that tonic meal of blood. During the millennium which immediately preceded the Christian era, and in the lands surrounding the Mediterranean Sea, ghosts were thin, shadowy, hardly personal beings. The dead survived, but wretchedly, faintly, as mere shadows. 'There is no work, nor device, nor knowledge, nor wisdom in Sheol, whither thou goest.' The words are from Ecclesiastes; but they might have been spoken almost anywhere in the Mediterranean world at almost any time between the Trojan war and the murder of Julius Caesar.

The squeak-and-gibber period of immortality came to an end, roughly speaking, at the beginning of the Christian era. Cicero and Virgil were still believers in the Homeric doctrines; they looked forward to a posthumous existence not more, but much less glorious than life on earth. 'Rather would I live on the ground as a hireling of another, with a landless man who had no great livelihood, than bear sway among the dead.' Their views were fundamentally the same as Homer's.

In this, they were not, for their age, very modern. For Plato and the mystagogues had already, long before, begun looking forward to a posthumous future very different from that which awaited the Homeric and Old Testament heroes. In Cicero's time, the squeak-and-gibber hypothesis was fast becoming antiquated. The rise of Christianity rendered it heretical as well as old-fashioned. The Christian dead were not allowed to squeak and gibber; they had either to sing and play the harp, or else to scream in never-ending agony. And they have continued to make music or scream until very recent times. In the course of the last century, however, very considerable changes have taken place. The fully Christian, fully personal, fully moral dead, with their music and their beatific vision, their deprivation of God's presence and their tortures, are now, I should guess, in the minority. What of the other departed? Many of them are simply non-existent; for the number of people who either dogmatically don't believe in, or else agnostically or uncaringly, simply don't bother about immortality is now considerable. Some, however, are glorious but impersonal survivors, reabsorbed, pantheistically, into a divine and universal Whole. Others again—the departed ones with whom certain spiritualists establish contacts, live on in an up-to-date version of the Red Indian's Happy Hunting Ground, a superior and slightly less material repetition of the present world complete with whiskies and sodas, cigars and midget golf-courses. The number of believers in this sort of survival seems to be increasing. Finally there is the scientific Psychical Researcher, whose views on the future life (if we may judge from the pronouncements of such eminent authorities as Professor C. E. Broad and M. René Sudre) seem to be almost indistinguishable from those held by Homer and the author of Ecclesiastes. For all that survives, according to these researchers (and the existing evidence, it seems to me, does not justify one in going any further) is what Professor Broad calls a 'psychic factor'—something which, in conjunction with a material brain, creates a personality but which, in isolation, is no more personal than matter. The dead, then, survive, but only fragmentarily, feebly, as mere wisps of floating memories. In a word, the squeak-and-gibber theory of survival is that which, according to some of the most competent scientific observers, best fits the available facts. Western thought has come back, where the question of immortality is concerned, to the point from which it started. And this is not surprising; for as Professor Leuba pointed out years ago in his excellent book, *The Belief in God and Immortality*, the Homeric conception of survival, the squeak-and-gibber theory as I have called it, is fundamentally scientific—a theory made to fit observable facts. Some of these facts, as we now see, were irrelevant to the question of survival. Others, however, were relevant.

The living sometimes have dreams of waking visions of the dead; sometimes, when they are thinking of the departed they experience the strange and singularly convincing 'sense of presence.' Ingenuous minds interpret such experiences in terms of a theory of survival

—a squeak-and-gibber theory; for it is the only one which fits this class of facts, just as it is the only one which fits the facts (if facts they are) of apparitions, hauntings, and the like. The modern psychical researcher bases his squeak-and-gibber theory on this latter class of 'super-normal' facts. The contemporaries of Homer based their similar theory on these same super-normalities (for presumably they manifested themselves then at least as often as they do now); but also on the quite irrelevant normalities of dream, vision, sense of presence, and the like. Old and new, both are scientific theories, that is to say, theories made to fit certain observed facts. The only difference between them is that the Homeric theorists accepted, as relevant, facts which we now see to have been beside the point. It happened, however, that their squeak-and-gibber theory fitted the irrelevant facts as neatly as it fitted and fits the relevant facts. So that their mistake was comparatively unimportant.

The Platonic and Christian theory of immortality —the harp-and-scream, as opposed to the squeak-and-gibber conception of a future life—is in no sense a scientific hypothesis. It was not created to fit observed facts; it was created to satisfy certain desires—some, of the most crassly selfish nature, others, the most loftily idealistic. The existence of these ideals and aspirations and even of these purely selfish longings for a continuance of personal being has been taken by many philosophers as the major premise of an argument, whose conclusion is the proved fact of personal and retributive immortality. But, as Broad has shown, it is hard (though not, in certain cases, impossible) to construct a logical bridge between the world of morality and the world of scientific truth; and anyhow, as a matter of historical fact, such bridges, when constructed, have almost invariably collapsed. Thus, the moral argument in favour of immortality will not bear the weight of scepticism. This logical bridge is a hopelessly ramshackle structure, and can be crossed only by those who wear the wings of faith and therefore have no real need of its support. As for the biological argument—that the existence of an inborn desire must imply the existence of an object of that desire, as hunger implies the existence of food and sexual desire that of a possible mate—this would be cogent only if the desire were universal. But it is not and has never been universal; the desire for survival is therefore not analogous to hunger or sexual appetite. Other philosophers have argued from the desire to the fact of immortality by asserting our incapacity even to conceive the cessation of our consciousness. This inconceivability of our own unconsciousness is a fact of psychology, upon which it is interesting and profitable to meditate. But since there is no difficulty at all in conceiving the cessation of other people's consciousness, I do not see that the argument derived from this fact can ever be wholly convincing. Immortality of the Platonic or Christian kind has been and must presumably remain the object only of hope, of longing, of faith; the survival, if survival it is, which is the object of scientific observation is survival of the Homeric kind— the squeak-and-gibber survival of shadowy and impersonal 'psychic factors.' By trying to interpret the facts of psychical research in terms of a modified Christian hypothesis, the spiritualists have involved themselves in inextricable difficulties. For the facts of psychical research simply do not warrant the adoption of anything remotely resembling a harp-and-scream conception of survival; the only rational interpretation to which they lend themselves is an interpretation in terms of some kind of squeak-and-gibber theory. Which is, admittedly, rather depressing. But then a great many things in this universe are rather depressing. Others, fortunately, are not. What we lose on the swings of pain, pointlessness, and evil, we gain on a variety of aesthetic, sensuous, intellectual, and moral roundabouts. Given a reasonable amount of luck, it is possible to live a not intolerable life. And if, afterwards, we find ourselves condemned to squeak and gibber, why, then, squeak and gibber we must. In the meantime let us make the best of rational speech.

One of the stock arguments in favour of Platonic and Christian immortality is this: if there were no future life, or at any rate no belief in future life, men would be justified in behaving like animals and, being justified, would all incontinently start taking the advice of Horace and the Preacher to do nothing but swill, guzzle, and copulate. Even a man of Dostoevsky's intelligence oracularly affirms that 'all things would be permitted' if there were no such thing as immortality. These moralists seem to forget that there are many human beings who simply don't want to pass their lives eating, drinking, and being merry, or, alternatively, like Russian heroes, raping, murdering, and morally torturing their friends. The deadly tedium of the Horatian and the nauseating unpleasantness of the Dostoevskyan life would be quite enough, survival or no survival, to keep me at any rate (in these matters one can only speak for oneself) unswervingly in the narrow way of domestic duty and intellectual labour. For the narrow way commands an incomparably wider, and, so far as I am concerned, an incomparably fairer prospect than the primrose path; fulfilled, domestic duties are a source of happiness, and intellectual labour is rewarded by the most intense delights. It is not the hope of heaven that prevents me from leading what is technically known as a life of pleasure; it is simply my temperament. I happen to find the life of pleasure boring and painful. And I should still find it boring and painful even if it were irrefragably proved to me that I was destined to be extinguished or, worse, to survive in the form of a squeaking and gibbering shade—as one of the 'weak heads,' in Homer's expressive phrase. *Nekuon amenena karena*—the weak heads of the dead. Those who have attended spiritualistic séances will agree that the description is painfully accurate.

BELIEFS AND ACTIONS

To the collectors of human specimens (a class to which I myself belong; for psychological varieties are the only things I have ever thought it worth while to collect) I recommend the two volumes of M. Jean Martet on the late Georges Clémenceau. One may not entirely approve of Clémenceau as a politician: one may even detest some of the principles and the methods of his statecraft. But in spite of this disapproval and hatred it is impossible not to admire the old tiger, it is impossible to withhold the homage due to a most extraordinary man. For after all there is nothing more admirable than Power—not the organized power of established society, which is generally detestable, but the native power of the individual, the daemonic energy of life. With this native inborn power, this living energy, Georges Clémenceau was richly endowed. A great man differs from common men by being, as it were, possessed by more than human spirits. These spirits may be good or evil; it is a matter almost of indifference. The important thing is that they should be more than human. It is the supernaturalness that makes the greatness and that we are forced to admire—even in the cases where the supernaturalness is morally evil and destructive. That Clémenceau was 'possessed' one cannot doubt. His devils may have worked in ways we disapprove of, to achieve ends which are not our ends, but they were genuine supernatural devils and, as such, worthy of all our admiration.

So much by way of somewhat irrelevant introduction to my theme. For my theme is not Georges Clémenceau. It is a theme of general psychological and historical interest which the ghost of Clémencaeu happened to suggest to me and of which the Tiger's career is a good illustration. For, reading M. Martet's book the other day I came upon the words recorded by him in the course of a conversation with the old statesman about the revolutionary socialists. 'These people,' said Clémenceau, 'do a lot of squealing so long as you allow them to squeal. But when you say "Shut up!" they shut up. ... They are mostly half-wits, and, what's more, they're hardly more courageous than the bourgeois—which is saying a good deal, my word! The thing that gives people courage is ideas. But these revolutionaries of yours have about as many ideas as my boots. Envy and resentment—that's all they've got. That sort of thing doesn't take you very far. I saw them during the war; I talked with them, I tried to find something in them; it's pitiable. I never had the smallest difficulty with these creatures.'

'The thing that gives people courage is ideas.' The phrase might be expanded. For it is not only courage that comes from ideas; it is determination; it is the power to act, the power to go on acting coherently. For though it is true that most ideas are the rationalizations of feelings, that does not mean that feelings are more important in the world of action than ideas. Feeling provides the original supply of energy, but this supply of energy soon fails if the feelings are not rationalized. For the rationalization justifies the feelings and serves at the same time both as a substitute for feelings and as a stimulant for them when they are dormant. You cannot go on feeling violently all the time—the human organism does not allow of it. But an idea persists; once you have persuaded yourself of its truth, an idea justifies the continuance in cold blood of actions which emotion could only have dictated in the heat of the moment. Indeed it does more than justify actions and feelings; it imposes them. If you accept an idea as true, then it becomes your duty to act on it even in cold blood as a matter not of momentary feeling, but of enduring principle. It is even your duty to revive the emotion which was originally at the root of the idea—or rather the new and nobler emotion which, thanks to the idea, has taken the place of the root feeling from which the idea started. Thus, to take an obvious example, envy—whether of the lucky in money or of the lucky in love—is constantly being rationalized in terms of political, economic, and ethical theory. For all those who cannot compete with him the successful amorist is a monster of immorality. The envied rich man is either wicked personally or vicariously wicked as the representative of an evil system. And having persuaded themselves of the iniquity of those they envy, the envious are not only justified in their now laudable hostility to the envied; they are also no longer envious. The idea has transformed their odious little personal feeling into a righteous indignation, a nobly disinterested love of virtue and abhorrence of wickedness. '*Ce qui donne du courage, ce sont les idées.*'

A question inevitably arises. What are the principal courage-giving, emotion-transforming, and action-inspiring ideas of the present epoch? They are certainly not the same as they were. Many of the great ideas which our ancestors accepted with little or no question are now only lukewarmly believed in or even rejected outright. Thus, the Christian, the specifically Catholic and Protestant ideas, once of such enormous significance and the source of so much creative and destructive action, have now lost a great deal of their potency. There are comparatively few men and women in the contemporary West who unquestionably rationalize their feelings in terms of the Christian philosophy and the Christian ethic, few who find in the old Christian ideas a source of courage and determination, a motive for prolonged and effective action. These religious ideas are not the only ones to have lost their force. There has been a decline in the effectiveness of certain political ideas, once immensely important. All the once inspiring ideas of nineteenth-century Liberalism are now without much power to move. It is only among the politically naïve and inexperienced populations of the East that we find them exerting anything like their ancient influence. The most powerful political idea at the present time is the idea of nationalism. It is the justifier and transformer of a whole host of emotions, the persisting motive of important individual and collective actions. Nationalism was the idea that gave old Clémenceau his ruthless and indomitable energy, '*Ce qui donne du courage, ce sont les idées.*' He knew it by personal experience.

The idea of progress is another of the great contemporary ideas. A vast amount of personal ambition, of rapacity, of lust for power is sanctified and at the same time made actively effective by this idea. It is in the idea of progress, coupled very often with the humanitarian idea of universal welfare and social service, that the modern business man finds excuses for his activities. Why does he work so hard? Why does he fight so ruthlessly against his rivals? To obtain power and make himself rich, the cynical realist would answer. Not at all, the business man indignantly replies, I am working and fighting for progress, for prosperity, for society.

There are signs, I believe, that this belief in progress and the ideas of humanitarianism is on the wane. The youngest generation seems to be less anxious than was its predecessor to justify its money-making and power-seeking in terms of these ideas. It affirms quite frankly that it works in order that it may be able to amuse itself in the intervals of leisure. The result of this rejection (it is still, of course, only a very partial rejection) of the inspiring ideas of an earlier generation is that the enthusiasm for work has perceptibly declined and that the amount of energy put into the money-making and power-seeking activities is less than it was. For it may be laid down as a general rule that any decline in the intensity of belief leads to a decline in effective activity.

And here, we find ourselves confronted with two

more questions. Is scepticism on the increase? and if so, what sort of new inspiring and justificatory ideas are men likely to accept in lieu of the old ideas in which they no longer believe? My impression is that we must answer yes to the first question. There is, I believe, a general increase in scepticism with regard to most of the hitherto accepted ideas, particularly in the sphere of ethics. There is a growing tendency to rely on momentary emotions as guides to conduct rather than on the fixed ideas in terms of which these emotions have hitherto been rationalized. The result is a general decline in the quality and quantity of activity among the sceptical.

In its extreme forms, however, scepticism is, for most human beings, intolerable. They must believe in something; they must have some sort of justificatory ideas. The contemporary circumstances (under which heading we must include recent political events, recent scientific discoveries, recent philosophical speculation) have forced on us a more or less complete scepticism with regard to most of the religious, ethical, and political ideas in terms of which our fathers could rationalize their feelings. For most of these ideas postulated the existence of certain transcendental entities. But it is precisely about these transcendental entities that modern circumstances compel us to feel sceptical. We find it difficult at the moment to believe in anything but untranscendental realities. (It is quite likely, of course, that this difficulty is only temporary and that a change of circumstances may reimpose belief in transcendental ideas. For the moment, however, we are sceptical about everything except the immediate.) In our daily lives the most important immediate realities are changing desires, emotions, moods. Some people accept these as they come and live from hand to mouth. But the 'realism' they profess is not only slightly sordid and ignoble; it is also sterile. It leaves them without courage, as Clémenceau would say, without the motive and the power to pursue a course of effective action. Many therefore seek for new justifying 'ideas' as a support and framework for their lives. These ideas, as we have seen, must not be in any way transcendental. The characteristically modern rationalization of feelings, desires, and moods is a rationalization in terms of the untranscendental—in terms, that is to say, of known psychology, not of postulated Gods, Virtues, Justices, and the like. The modern emphasis is on personality. We justify our feelings and moods by an appeal to the 'right to happiness,' the 'right to self-expression.' (This famous 'right to self-expression,' unthinkable in days when men firmly believed that they had duties to God, has done enormous mischief in the sphere of education.) In other words, we claim to do what we like, not because doing what we like is in harmony with some supposed absolute good, but because it is good in itself. A poor justification and one which is hardly sufficient to make men courageous and active. And yet modern circumstances are such that it is only in terms of this sort of 'idea' that we can hope successfully to rationalize our emotional and impulsive behaviour. My own feeling is that these untranscendental rationalizations can be improved. It is possible, as Blake said, to see infinity in a grain of sand and eternity in a flower. Only in terms of such an idea, it seems to me, can the modern man satisfactorily 'rationalize' (though the idea is mystically irrational) his feelings and impulses. Whether such rationalizations are as good, pragmatically speaking, as the old rationalizations in terms of transcendental entities, I do not know. On the whole, I rather doubt it. But they are the best, it seems to me, that the modern circumstances will allow us to make.

NOTES ON LIBERTY AND THE BOUNDARIES OF THE PROMISED LAND

'MEDIAEVAL liberty,' said Lord Acton, 'differs from modern in this, that it depended on property.' But the difference is surely a difference only in degree, not in kind. Money may have less influence in a modern than in a mediaeval court of law. But outside the court of law? Outside, it is true, I am legally free to work or not to work, as I choose; for I am not a serf. I am legally free to live here rather than there; for I am not bound to the land. I am free, within reasonable limits, to amuse myself as I like; archdeacons do not fine me for indulging in what they consider unseemly diversions. I am legally free to marry any one (with the possible exception of a member of the royal family) from my first cousin to the daughter of a duke; no lord compels me to marry a girl or widow from the manor, no priest forbids the banns within the seventh degree of consanguinity.

The list of all my legal freedoms would run to pages of type. Nobody in all history has been so free as I am now.

But let us see what happens if I try to make use of my legal liberty. Not a serf, I choose to stop working; result, I shall begin to starve next Monday. Not bound to the land, I elect to live in Grosvenor Square and Taormina; unhappily, the rent of my London house alone amounts to five times my yearly income. Not subject to persecutions of ecclesiastical busybodies, I decide that it would be pleasant to take a young woman to the Savoy for a bite of supper; but I have no dress clothes, and I should spend more on my evening's entertainment than I can earn in a week. Not bound to marry at the bidding of a master, free to choose wherever I like, I decide to look for a bride at Chatsworth or Welbeck; but when I ring the bell, I am told to go round to the servants' entrance and look sharp about it.

All my legal liberties turn out in practice to be as closely dependent on property as were the liberties of my mediaeval ancestors. The rich can buy large quantities of freedom; the poor must do without it, even though, by law and theoretically, they have as good a right to just as much of it as have the rich.

A right is something which I have at the expense of other people. Even my right of not being murdered and not being made a slave is something which I have at the expense of those stronger than myself who could kill me or force me into servitude. There are no such things as 'natural rights'; there are only adjustments of conflicting claims. What I have at your expense ought not to be more than what you have at my expense: that, whatever the practice may be, is the theory of Justice.

Many murderees and slaves, however feeble, are stronger, in the last resort, than a few slavers and murderers. From time to time the slaves and murderees have actually demonstrated this in sanguinary fashion. These revolts, though rare, though quite astonishingly rare (the abject patience of the oppressed is perhaps the most inexplicable, as it is also the most important, fact in all history) have been enough to scare the oppressors into making considerable concessions, not only in theory, but even in practice.

Legally and theoretically, we are all free now; but the right to make use of these liberties must continue, under the present dispensation, to depend on property and the personal abilities which enable a man to acquire property easily. Some people, like tramps and certain artists, enjoy, it is true, a good deal of liberty without paying for it; but this is only because, unlike most human beings, they are not interested to stake out a claim among the things which can be paid for with money.

In the egalitarian state of the future all excessive

accumulations of property will be abolished. But this implies, apparently, the abolition of all excessive enjoyment of liberty. When everybody has three hundred a year, nobody will be less, but also nobody presumably will be more, free than the contemporary confidential clerk. 'But in the future state,' say the prophets, 'three hundred a year will buy five thousand pounds' worth of liberty.' And when we ask how, by what miracle? they invoke, not the god from the machine, but the machine itself.

Every right, as we have seen, is something which we have at other people's expense. The machine is the only 'other person' at whose expense we can have things with a good conscience and also the only 'other person' who becomes steadily more and more efficient.

Served by mechanical domestics, exploiting the incessant labour of metallic slaves, the three-hundred-a-year man of the future state will enjoy an almost indefinite leisure. A system of transport, rapid, frequent, and cheap, will enable him to move about the globe more freely than the migrant *rentier* of the present age. Nor need he forgo (except in private) the rich man's privilege of living luxuriously. Already mass production has made it possible for the relatively poor to enjoy elaborate entertainments in surroundings of more than regal splendour. The theatres in which the egalitarians will enjoy the talkies, tasties, smellies, and feelies, the Corner Houses where they will eat their synthetic poached eggs on toast-substitute and drink their surrogates of coffee, will be prodigiously much vaster and more splendid than anything we know to-day. Compared with them, the hall of Belshazzar in Martin's celebrated picture will seem the squalidest of little chop-houses, and Bibbiena's palaces, Piranesi's imaginary Roman temples, mere dog-holes, hutches, and sties.

Urbs Sion unica, mansio mystica, condita coelo (or rather
    mundo).
Nunc tibi gaudeo, nunc tibi lugeo, tristor, anhelo. . . .
Opprimit omne cor ille tuus decor, o Sion, o pax.
Urbs sine tempore, nulla potest fore laus tibi mendax.
O nova mansio, te pia concio, gens pia munit,
Provehit, excitat, auget, identitat, efficit, unit.

Well, let's hope that this *mansio mystica* will prove to be as jolly as its prophets say that it looks. Let's hope in particular that its inhabitants will enjoy their universal egalitarian liberties as much as we enjoy the little freedoms which the present dispensation allows us unjustly to buy or punishes us for criminally stealing.

My own hopes are tempered, I must confess, with certain doubts. For there's a divinity, as I see, that misshapes as well as one that shapes our ends. Suitably enough (for like bad dogs, bad gods deserve bad names), this malignant deity is called the Law of Diminishing Returns. It was the economists who gave him the name and who first recognized and clearly described his unfriendly activities. But it would be a mistake to suppose that this demon confines himself solely to the economic sphere. The law of diminishing returns holds good in almost every part of our human universe.

Here, for example, is a very melancholy man who starts drinking Burgundy with his dinner. His melancholy soon wears off and is replaced by cheerfulness, which increases steadily with every drop of Burgundy consumed, until, three-quarters of the way through his first bottle, a maximum is reached. He goes on drinking; but the next half-bottle produces no perceptible alteration in his condition; he remains where he was —at the top of his high spirits. A few more glasses, however, and his cheerfulness begins once more to decline. He becomes first quarrelsome, then lachrymose, and finally feels most horribly unwell and therefore miserable. He is worse off at the end of his second bottle than he was on an empty stomach.

Similarly, beyond a certain point the return in happiness of increased prosperity steadily diminishes. This is an ancient commonplace. It is only our lingering belief in the eighteenth-century heresy of perfectibility that makes us still loath to admit the hardly less obvious facts about education. For education is as much subject to the end-misshaping law as wine, or prosperity, or artificial manure. Increase in the amount or intensity of training gives returns in the form of increased mental efficiency and moral excellence; but after a certain maximum (which varies for each individual) has been passed, these returns steadily diminish and may even take on a negative value. Thus the oblate children in mediaeval monasteries were subject to a long and Spartan training in virtue. 'Children should ever have chastisement with custody and custody with chastisement,' says the author of the constitutions of Cluny; and for a century or two the oblates got these things—with a vengeance. But the system broke down; for as a conscientious abbot complained to St. Anselm, 'we cease not to chastise our boys by day and by night, yet they grow daily worse and worse.' The returns of education had diminished to the point of becoming negative.

Much the same thing happens in the sphere of politics. The democratization of political institutions gives returns in the form of increased justice and increased social efficiency. A peak is reached, and, if the process goes any further, the returns begin to diminish. In Italy, for example, just after the introduction of proportional representation, their values were rapidly ceasing to be positive. Hence, among other reasons, the rise of Fascism.

What has the end-misshaping divinity to say about liberty? Let us consider a few particular cases and try to guess how the god will pronounce himself on each.

'Perfected machinery,' say the prophets, 'will give us increasing freedom from work, and increasing freedom from work will give increasing happiness.' But leisure also is subject to the law of diminishing returns. Beyond a certain point, more freedom from work produces a diminished return in happiness. Among the completely leisured, the returns in happiness are often actually negative and acute boredom is suffered. As soon, moreover, as they are freed from the servitude of labour, many leisured people voluntarily abandon themselves to a servitude of amusement and social duties, more pointless than work and often quite as arduous. Will the leisured majority of the egalitarian world be different in character from the leisured few to-day? Only the eugenists have any reason to suppose so.

Consider another point often insisted upon by the prophets of Utopia. 'Travel,' they say (and with reason), 'is a liberal education. Freedom to travel has been a privilege reserved to the rich. Leisure, with cheap and rapid transport, will make this privilege accessible to all.

Therefore all will receive the liberal education which only a few were once at liberty to enjoy.' Once more, however, the end-misshaping divinity intervenes. Travel is educative because it brings the traveller into contact with people of different culture from his own, living under alien conditions. But the more travelling there is, the more will culture and way of life tend everywhere to be standardized and therefore the less educative will travel become. There is still some point in going from Burslem to Udaipur. But when all the inhabitants of Burslem have been sufficiently often to Udaipur and all the inhabitants of Udaipur have been sufficiently often to Burslem, there will be no point whatever in making the journey. Leaving out of account a few trifling geological and climatic idiosyncrasies, the two towns will have become essentially indistinguishable.

'Nature uplifts; the sublime and the beautiful are moralizing and spiritualizing forces. In Utopia all men will have the means, financial and mechanical, to make themselves familiar with the beauties and sublimities of nature.' But, as I have remarked elsewhere, only such peoples as dislike the country possess any country to dislike. Nations that love the country destroy what they adore. Witness the two thousand square miles of London's suburbs. Beauty-spots accessible to whole populations cease to be beauty-spots and become Blackpools.

Liberty depends on property; when few had property, only a few were free to go and seek inspiration or solace among the 'Beauties of Nature.' In the egalitarian state all will have property or its communistic equivalent. All will therefore be free to go and inspire or solace themselves in the country. But the greater the number which avails itself of this liberty, the less will this liberty be worth. And this would seem to be true, not only of travel and the pleasures of country life, but of practically all the privileges and freedoms hitherto reserved to the few. We have seen that, after a certain point, any increase in the amount of liberty brings a diminishing return of happiness; so also, it would seem, does any increase in what may be called liberty's area of incidence.

A conclusion imposes itself. Continuous general progress (along present lines) is only possible upon two conditions: that the heritable qualities of the progressing population shall be improved (or at any rate changed in a specific direction) by deliberate breeding; and that the amount of population shall be reduced.

Increase of material prosperity, increase of leisure, increase of liberty, increase of educational facilities are perfectly useless to individuals, in whom every such increase beyond a quickly reached maximum gives diminishing returns of happiness, virtue, and intellectual efficiency. Only by raising the critical point, at which increase of goods begins to give diminishing psychological returns, can we make continuous progress a reality for the individual and, through the individual, for society at large. How can we raise this critical point? By deliberate breeding and selection. At any rate, no other method offers us the least prospect of success.

So much for the first condition of continuous progress; now for the second. Certain experiences, we agree, are valuable. They are enjoyed at present by a few privileged human beings; it would be a progress in the sphere of social justice if they could be enjoyed by all. But, as we have seen, to extend privileges is generally to destroy their value. Experiences which, enjoyed by a few, were precious, cease automatically to be precious when enjoyed by many. A certain number of these precious experiences might be made accessible to all the members of a population provided that it were sufficiently small. (For example, where populations are small, beauty-spots need not become Blackpools.) In these cases progress can only become a reality to the individual on condition that the progressing community, of which he is a member, is absolutely small. Where the community is large, its numbers must be reduced.

There are other cases, however, in which the precious experiences could never be made accessible to whole populations, however small, absolutely. For in these cases the preciousness of the experience is found to consist precisely in the fact that it can only be enjoyed by a minority. To provide such experiences, it will be necessary in any future egalitarian society to create a number of mutually exclusive clubs or, better, secret societies, religious sects, even witches' covens. Only by such means can the members of an egalitarian society be made free of the infinitely precious experience of being in a superior minority.

ON THE CHARMS OF HISTORY AND THE FUTURE OF THE PAST

THERE are best sellers now among the history books, and archaeology is actually news. From an editor's point of view, the finding of yet another of Tutankhamen's hideous *art nouveau* table-centres is an event at least as important as an Atlantic flight. We are all interested in history now.

But 'history,' Mr. Henry Ford assures us, 'is bunk.' Therefore, if Mr. Ford is right, we are all interested in bunk. Is he right? Up to a point, I think, he is. For most of what passes for history is really perfectly insignificant and trivial. Why, then, are we interested in it? Because we like insignificances and trivialities—prefer them (bottomlessly frivolous as we are) to the significant things which demand to be taken seriously, to be judged and thought about. Moreover, historical insignificances and trivialities, besides being intrinsically delightful (a history book is often more entertaining than a novel), are also Culture. We are therefore morally justified in being amused by them, as we are not morally justified in being amused by novels. For novels, unless they happen to be by dead writers, are not Culture.

Culture, as Emmanuel Berl has pointed out in one of his brilliantly entertaining pamphlets, is like the sum of special knowledge that accumulates in any large united family and is the common property of all its members. 'Do you remember Aunt Agatha's ear trumpet? And how Willie made the parrot drunk with sops in wine? And that picnic on Loch Etive, when the boat upset and Uncle Bob was nearly drowned? Do you remember?' And we all do; and we laugh delightedly; and the unfortunate stranger, who happens to have called, feels utterly out of it. Well, that (in its social aspects) is Culture. When we of the great Culture Family meet, we exchange reminiscences about Grandfather Homer, and that awful old Dr. Johnson, and Aunt Sappho, and poor Johnny Keats. 'And do you remember that absolutely priceless thing Uncle Virgil said? You know. *Timeo Danaos* . . . Priceless; I shall never forget it.' No, we shall never forget it; and what's more, we shall take good care that those horrid people who have had the impertinence to call on us, those wretched outsiders who never knew dear mellow old Uncle V, shall never forget it either. We'll keep them constantly reminded of their outsideness. So pleasurable to members of the Culture Family is this rehearsal of tribal gossip, such a glow of satisfied superiority does it give them, that the *Times* finds it profitable to employ some one to do nothing else but talk to us every morning about our dear old Culture-Aunties and -Uncles and their delightful friends. Those fourth leading articles are really extraordinary. 'How the days draw in!' as the Swan of Litchfield used mournfully to exclaim. The sere and yellow leaf, the *sanglots longs des violons de l'automne* fill some hearts with a certain 'sweet sorrow' and bring to some eyes the *lacrimae rerum*. But there are others—*quot homines, tot disputandum est*—who find the 'season of mists and mellow fruitfulness' not only cheering, but actually, unlike poor Cowper's afternoon cup, inebriating. For 'give to the boys October!' as we used to sing in the Auld Lang Syne of our Harrow days. Sad recollections! *Nessun maggior dolore che ricordarsi del tempo felice nella miseria.* Those beautiful lines of Lactantius rise spontaneously to the lips:

> *A ab absque, coram, de;*
> *Palam clam, cum ex et e;*
> *Sine tenus, pro et prae. . . .*

I confess, I thoroughly enjoy reading this sort of thing when it is well put together. I take a real pleasure in recognizing some Culture-Uncle's quip, and am overcome with shame when I read of avuncular words or exploits, with which I ought to be familiar, but inexcusably am not. I am even very fond of writing this sort of family gossip myself.

All the more picturesque figures of history are our Culture-Uncles and Culture-Aunties. If you can talk knowingly about their sayings and doings, it is a sign that you 'belong,' that you are one of the family. Whereas if you don't know, for example, that 'Sidney's sister, Pembroke's mother' was fond of watching the mating of her mares and stallions, if you don't know that Harrington was convinced that his perspiration engendered flies and actually devised a crucial experiment to prove it—well, obviously, you're a bit of an outsider.

To pass the time and to provide us with Culture-Uncles and Culture-Aunts—these, for most readers, are the two main functions of written history. Mr. Ford calls it bunk—no wonder. We can only be surprised at his moderation. Working single-mindedly *ad majorem Industriae gloriam* (as our Culture-Uncle Loyola might have said), this ascetic missionary and saint of the new dispensation could not fail to hate history. For the reading of history distracts, is a time-killer—thanks to

Culture, an accredited and legitimate time-killer; but time is a sacrifice reserved exclusively for the God of Industry. Again, history provides people with standards of culture-snobbery; but the only kind of snobbery permitted to a worshipper of the new divinity is the snobbery of possessions. The God of Industry supplies his worshippers with objects and can only exist on condition that his gifts are gratefully accepted. In the eyes of an Industriolater the first duty of man is to collect as many objects as he can. Family pride in the possession of Culture-Uncles, and in general all culture-snobbery, interferes with pride in objects, or possession-snobbery. Culture-snobbery is an insult and even a menace to the God of Industry.

The Saint of the new dispensation has no choice but to hate history. And not history only. If he is logical he must hate literature, philosophy, pure science, the arts—all the mental activities that distract mankind from an acquisitive interest in objects.

'Bunk' was the term of abuse selected by Mr. Ford for disparaging history. Bunk: for how can even serious and philosophical history be enlightening? History is the account of people who lived before such things as machine tools and joint-stock banks had been invented. How can it say anything of significance to us, in whose lives machine tools and joint-stock banks play, directly or indirectly, such an enormous part? No, no. History is bunk.

There are arguments, good arguments, I think, against the presumed bunkiness of history. But I cannot go into them here. Here, I am concerned simply with the fact that, bunk or no bunk, we all find history interesting. Interesting because it delightfully kills time, justifies time-killing by being Culture, and, finally, because it deals precisely with those pre-machine-tool men whose actions must seem to any convinced industriolater so ridiculously irrelevant and beside the point. We read about the past, because the past is refreshingly different from the present. A great deal of history is written, whether deliberately or unconsciously, as wish-fulfilment.

The past and the future are functions of the present. Each generation has its private history, its own peculiar brand of prophecy. What it shall think about past and future is determined by its own immediate problems. It will go to the past for instruction, for sympathy, for justification, for flattery. It will look into the future for compensation for the present—into the past, too. For even the past can become a compensatory Utopia, indistinguishable from the earthly paradises of the future, except by the fact that the heroes have historical names and flourished between known dates. From age to age the past is recreated. A new set of Waverley Novels is founded on a new selection of the facts. The Waverley Novels of one age are about the Romans, of another about the Greeks, of a third about the Crusaders or the Ancient Chinese.

The future is as various as the past. The coming world is inhabited at one moment by politicians, at another by craftsmen and artists; now by perfectly rational utilitarians, now by supermen, now by proletarian sub-men. Each generation pays its money and takes its choice.

Anywhere, anywhere out of the world. We make our exit, forward or backward, by time-machine. (Some people, it is true, still prefer the old-fashioned eternity-machines on which Dante and Milton made their record-breaking trans-cosmic flights; but they are relatively few. For most moderns, the time-machine seems unquestionably more efficient.) Shall we always make the same sort of exits on our time-machines? In other words, what is likely to be the future of the past? And the future of the future? Only a study of the past's and future's past and present will permit us to guess with any show of plausibility.

For the five or six hundred years before 1800 the past was almost exclusively Rome, Greece (known indirectly through Rome and then by direct contact), and Palestine.

The Hebrew past remained, throughout all this long period, relatively stable. Associated as it was with the sacred books of the established religion, how could it change?

The Graeco-Roman past was less stable. During the later Middle Ages the Greeks and Romans were, above all, men of science. With the Renaissance appeared that passionate and exclusive admiration for classical art and literature which persisted until well on into the nineteenth century. For more than three hundred years, the Greeks and Romans were the only sculptors and architects, the only poets, dramatists, philosophers, and historians.

During the same period the Romans were the only statesmen.

For the sceptics of the eighteenth century, Greece and Rome were empires of Reason, gloriously unlike the actual world, where prejudice and superstition so manifestly had the upper hand. They used classical examples as sticks with which to beat the priests and kings, as levers with which to overturn the current morality. And they did not confine themselves exclusively to Greece and Rome. It was at this time that China was first held up as an example of sweet reasonableness to shame the benighted folly of the West. In beating the West with an extreme-oriental stick, contemporary writers like Lowes Dickinson and Bertrand Russell have only revived a most respectable literary tradition. The primitive and prehistoric Utopias of D. H. Lawrence and Elliott Smith have as good a pedigree. Our ancestors knew all about the State of Nature and the Noble Savage.

The last years of the eighteenth century and the first of the nineteenth were a period of rapid and violent change. The past changed with the present; Greece and Rome took on a succession of new meanings. For the men of the French Revolution they were important in so far as they connoted republicanism and tyrannicide. For Napoleon, Greece was Alexander, and Rome, Augustus and Justinian. In Germany, meanwhile, attention was mainly concentrated on Greece. Greece, for the contemporaries of Schiller and Goethe, was a world of art, above all a world where men lived a rich individual life. It is difficult, as Rousseau pointed out, to be at once a citizen and a man. He who would become a good citizen of a modern society must sacrifice some of his most precious and fundamental human impulses. Where there is too much specialization, too much of the organized division of labour, a man is easily degraded to the level of a mere embodied function. It was the realization of this that sent Schiller and Goethe back to the Greeks. Among the Greeks they thought they could discover the fully and harmoniously developed individual man.

The fall of Napoleon was followed by religious and political reaction. Inevitably, the Middle Ages made their appearance upon the mental scene. During the first half of the century the Middle Ages fulfilled the wishes of three distinct classes of people—of the temperamental romantics, who found the new industrialism squalid and pined for passion and picturesqueness; of the missionary Christians who pined for universal faith; of the aristocrats who pined for political and economic privileges.

Later on, when industrialism and the policy of *laissez-faire* had had time to produce their most dreadful results, the Middle Ages began to connote something rather different. The wish-fulfilling world to which William Morris and his friends looked back was picturesque, indeed, but not particularly catholic or feudal; it was a world, above all, of sound economic organization, a pre-mechanical world, peopled by not too highly specialized artist-craftsmen.

Of all the various pasts the mediaeval is still one of the most lively. It has inspired several contemporary politico-economic ideals, of which one, the Fascist version of Guild Socialism, has actually been converted into a practical policy and applied. It is looked back to yearningly by enemies of capitalism, such as Tawney, by enemies of democracy, such as Maurras, by enemies of the overgrown industrial state, such as Belloc and Chesterton, by all the artistic enemies of mass production, by Catholics, Socialists, Monarchists alike. Only in a confused and complicated present could a piece of the past simultaneously mean so many different things.

But the mediaeval is by no means the only past in which we take a wish-fulfilling interest. Thus, a fabulously spiritual Indian past has been invented by the theosophists to compensate ideally for the far from spiritual Western present. Again, Greece is the retrospective Utopia of those who, like Schiller, find that the citizenship of a modern state is dehumanizing. (Ever since Nietzsche's denunciation of Socrates, the Greek Utopia has been pre-Platonic. Platonic and post-Platonic Greece is too modern to be a really satisfactory world of wish-fulfilments. The Hellenistic age was, in many respects, quite horrifyingly like our own.) The archaeological discoveries of the last twenty years have opened up a very glorious receding vista of new Utopias. Crete and Mycenae and Etruria, Ur and the Indus valley have become what I may call Popular Historical Resorts—Holiday Haunts for Tired Business Men. Almost no weapons have been found at Harappa. For that alone our war-wounded world must love and cherish it.

And finally there are the savages—not even noble ones now; we almost prefer them ignoble. Physically our contemporaries, but mentally belonging to a culture much more ancient, much less advanced than that of Ur or Harappa, the few remaining primitive peoples of the earth have achieved a prodigious popularity among those who have wishes to fulfil—a popularity about which Mr. Wyndham Lewis, in his *Pale Face*, probably does well to be angry.

So much for the past of the past and the present of the past; what about the future of the past? It seems fairly obvious that the major problems of our generation will continue to be the major problems of the two or three generations succeeding our own. Our industrial, political, and social difficulties are nowhere near solution, and can hardly, in the nature of things, be solved in a short time. The immediate future of the past will therefore, in all probability, resemble its present. In the many mansions of the Middle Ages political and social reformers will continue, no doubt, to discover each one his own snug little Utopia, feudal, Socialist, or Catholic. With every increase in proletarian irreligion the spirituality of the ancient East will be heightened. An India of navel-gazers and squinters at nose-tips is likely to become as popular as, among the noises and imbecile hustlings of future cities, an ancient China full of beautifully leisured mandarins and rational Confucians.

If society continues to develop on its present lines, specialization is bound to increase. Men will come to be valued more and more, not as individuals, but as personified social functions. The result of this will be a heightened interest in the Greeks and in any other historical personages who may be supposed to have led a full, harmonious life as individuals, not as cogs in an industrial machine. But Greeks and even Cretans and Harappans will not be enough in this coming age of intensive specialization and more and more meaningless routine. There is likely, in spite of Mr. Lewis, to be a growing admiration of primitives. (As actual primitives disappear under the influence of drink and syphilis on the one hand and of education on the other, this admiration for them will tend to increase; the most satisfactory ideals are those that have no actual fancy-cramping embodiments.) With every advance of industrial civilization the savage past will be more and more appreciated, and the cult of D. H. Lawrence's *Dark God* may be expected to spread through an ever-widening circle of worshippers.

In making this prophecy I have deliberately neglected to consider the possible effects upon the readers and writers of future history books of eventual progress in the science of history itself. Our knowledge of the past tends steadily to increase. Some of these increases of knowledge confirm our traditional conceptions of the past; others, on the contrary, impose upon us new ways of thinking. From time to time the scholar and the retrospective Utopist come into conflict. Those who enjoy gladiatorial shows will remember with pleasure the recent fight between Mr. G. K. Chesterton and Mr. Coulton on the subject of mediaeval puritanism. Being a good Catholic and a romantic believer in the actual existence of a mediaeval Merry England, even a Merry Europe, for ever ruined by a gang of revolting Calvinists and Independents, Mr. Chesterton was naturally distressed when Mr. Coulton began piling up evidence to prove the intense puritanism of official Catholic Christianity during the Middle Ages. Armed with his usual eloquence and a cautious statement by St. Thomas to the effect that all dancers are not necessarily damned, he rushed into the arena. Mr. Coulton, who has had the bad taste to read all the documents, repulsed the attack with another shower of puritanical quotations. The impartial spectator was forced to conclude that if England was ever merry it was not because of official Catholicism, but in spite of the Church's constant denunciation of merriment. Mr. Chesterton's particular brand of retrospective Utopism is henceforth untenable. Conscientious Merry-Englanders will have to put Mr. Coulton on the index. Many other comforting visions of the past will certainly vanish, as knowledge spreads. My own impression is that the earthly paradise will steadily be pushed back and back into the unknown and unknowable ages of pre-history. Knowledge will turn out so regularly to be a knowledge of mainly unpleasant facts that the Utopists will be compelled in mere self-defence to take refuge either in deliberate ignorance of what is known, or else in the comfortable darkness beyond the fringes of recorded history.

Prophecy is more closely dependent on the present than history. A man living in the petrol age can quite easily reconstruct for himself the life of a man living in the horse age. But a man of the horse age could not be expected to foresee the petrol-man's mode of life. It would be easy but quite uninteresting to catalogue the errors of past prophets. The only significant parts of their prognostications, the only parts of them which we can usefully compare with contemporary prophesyings are the forecasts of political and social organization. Coaches may give place to aeroplanes, but man remains very much what he was—a mainly gregarious animal endowed with a certain number of anti-social instincts.

Whatever tools he uses, however slowly or quickly he may travel, he must always be governed and regimented.

I lack the time and the learning to describe the entire historical past of the future. It will be enough for my purpose in this essay to give a summary description of the sort of future thought possible and desirable by the men of the eighteenth and early nineteenth centuries, and to compare it with the futures thought possible and desirable to-day. (For travellers on time-machines desirable futures are limited to the category of possibility. Travellers on eternity-machines are free, of course, to choose the impossibly desirable.)

For our ancestors, as for ourselves, the future was compensatory. They called in new worlds to redress the balance of the old. They corrected present evils prophetically. The future Utopias of Helvétius, Lemercier, and Babeuf, of Godwin and Shelley, have a certain family resemblance among themselves. Democracy in those days was not the bedraggled and rather whorish old slut she now is, but young and attractive. Her words persuaded. When she spoke of the native equality and potential perfection of human beings, men believed her. For Shelley and his philosophical masters, vice and stupidity were the fruits of ignorance and despotic government. Get rid of priests and kings, make Aeschylus and the differential calculus accessible to all, and the world will become a paradise and every human being a saint and a genius, or at the very least a stoic philosopher.

We have had experience of the working of democracy, we have seen the fruits of universal education, and we have come to doubt the premises from which our ancestors started out on their prophetic argument. Psychology and genetics have yielded results which confirm the doubts inspired by practical experience. Nature, we have found, does rather more, nurture rather less, to make us what we are than the earlier humanitarians had supposed. We believe in Mendelian predestination; and in a society not practising eugenics, Mendelian predestination leads as inevitably to pessimism about the temporal future as Augustinian or Calvinistic predestination leads to pessimism about the eternal future.

Contemporary prophets have visions of future societies founded on the idea of natural inequality, not of natural equality; they look forward to the re-establishment, on a new and much more realistic foundation, of the old hierarchies; they have visions of a ruling aristocracy and of a race slowly improved, not by any improvement in the educational, legal, or physical environment (incapable, however effective for promoting present happiness, of altering the quality of the stock), but by deliberate eugenic breeding.

Such is our present future. It is reasonable to suppose that the future future of our immediate descendants will be of the same kind as our own, but modified in its details. Thus we can imagine our children having visions of a new caste system based on differences in native ability and accompanied by a Machiavellian system of education, designed to give the members of the lower castes only such instruction as it is profitable for society at large and the upper castes in particular that they should have. Their children's children will perhaps be in a position clearly to foresee a future, in which eugenic breeding will have falsified these prophecies by abolishing the lower castes altogether. What will happen then? But the distant future of the future is really too remote to be profitably discussed.

SECTION III

OBSTACLE RACE

Armance, if not one of the best, is certainly the queerest of all Stendhal's writings: the queerest and, for me at any rate, one of the most richly suggestive. It is the history of the unhappy loves of two young people, members of that strange society of *Ultras* which flourished, briefly and anachronistically, under the restored Bourbons. Aristocrats, Armance and Octave are also noble by temperament and intimate conviction; they have 'well-born souls.' Hence their unhappiness. They love one another; but their relations are simply a long series of misunderstandings—misunderstandings which can never be explained away, since each is bound to silence by the dictates now of religion, now of social convention, now of a categorically imperative code of honour. Moreover, poor Octave has a private source of misery all his own. What it is we are never told. All we know is that the young man bears the burden of an awful secret—a secret that makes him behave at moments like a dangerous lunatic, that plunges him at other times into the blackest melancholy. What is this secret? Armance actually brings herself to ask the indelicate question; and after a terrible inward struggle Octave sets down the answer in a briefly worded note. But there is yet another misunderstanding, brought about this time by their enemies. At the last moment Octave decides not to post his letter. Its contents remain for ever undivulged, not only to Armance, but even to the inquisitive reader. However, the inquisitive reader, if he is also a perspicacious reader, will by this time have guessed what that fatal note contained; and his guess finds itself confirmed by certain earlier readers, friends of the author, who applied to Stendhal himself for an answer to the riddle and have recorded his reply. Octave, poor devil, was impotent. His well-born soul was lodged in a, physiologically speaking, ill-born body.

Born a century later, how would Octave and Armance behave themselves to-day? It is amusing, it is also deeply instructive, to speculate. To start with, they would be at liberty to see one another as much as they liked. No social conventions, no inward scruples of religion would prevent Armance (who, as an orphan with a small independent income, would almost certainly be studying Art, or taking courses at the London School of Economics) from accepting all Octave's invitations to walk and talk, to dine and (for this is the Age of Prohibition) wine, to go motoring with him into the country and even to accompany him for week-ends to Paris, fortnights to Spain or Sicily. (*En tout bien, tout honneur*, of course. In this particular case, it is true, it could hardly be otherwise. But in our days *bien* and *honneur* will often remain intact, even when the young man is not afflicted with poor Octave's disability, even when the season is spring and the scene Taormina or Granada. And when they don't remain intact, who cares, after all?)

Stendhal's hero and heroine had as little liberty of speech as they had of action. Not only did the conventions keep them physically apart; it was also morally impossible for them to talk openly about almost any matter which they felt to be vitally important. Octave was rich, Armance poor and proud. Delicacy and a convention of honour did not permit them to talk about money. And yet it was the disparity of their fortunes which made Armance reluctant to admit her love for Octave—so reluctant, that she invented a phantom fiancé to keep him at a distance. They were condemned to suffer in silence and because of silence. Silence, again, impenetrably surrounded poor Octave's secret. Christian modesty forbade its discussion; and even if Octave had actually posted the note, in which, after so much inward wrestling, he had divulged the dreadful truth, would Armance have understood a word of it? Certainly not, if she had been well brought up. To-day there would be no inward impediment to their working out the financial problem, with its moral corollaries, down to the last, most practical details. Nor is it in the least difficult for us to imagine two young contemporaries discussing the still more intimate questions raised by Octave's disability—whether it were best treated by psychoanalysis or electricity, whether, if it proved incurable, marriage would be possible and, if so, on what conditions. . . .

Poor Octave! Unhappy Armance! Their whole life was a kind of obstacle race—a climbing over and a crawling under barriers, a squeezing through narrow places. And the winning-post? For Octave the winning-post was an overdose of laudanum; for Armance, a cell in a nunnery.

If they had run their race to-day, they would have run it on the flat, or at any rate over a course irregular only by nature, not artificially obstructed. The going is easier now. But are they entirely to be pitied, are we to be congratulated without reserve? And the notion of turning life into an obstacle race—is that so wholly bad? Isn't plain flat racing just a little boring—not merely for the spectators, but even for the runners themselves?

The flattest racing in the world, at any rate in the sphere of sexual relationships, is modern Russian racing. I have never been in Russia, and must depend for my information on books. One of the best of these informative books is the collection of short stories by Romanof, recently translated into English under the title, *Without Cherry Blossom*. The theme of almost all these stories is fundamentally the same—the depressing flatness of amorous flat racing. And, heavens, how intolerably flat it must be in a country where souls have been abolished by official decree, where 'psychology' is a term of abuse and being in love is disparaged as merely 'mental'! 'For us,' says one of Romanof's women students, 'love does not exist; we have only sexual relationships. And so, love is scornfully relegated to the realm of "psychology," and our right to existence is only understood physiologically. . . . And any one who is trying to find in love anything beyond the physiological is laughed down as mental or a bad case.'

Elsewhere, the racing is by no means as flat as it is in Russia. And let us remember that in Russia it is flat only where sex is concerned. In other spheres, Communism has probably erected more obstacles than it pulled down. For to erect obstacles is one of the principal functions of religion (according to Salomon Reinach, the only function); and Communism is one of the few actively flourishing religions of the modern world. Our non-sexual racing is probably flatter than the corresponding thing in Communist Russia. And anyhow, sexual or non-sexual, compared with the fantastic steeple-chasing imposed by convention and Catholicism on the protagonists of Stendhal's little tragedy, it seems positively an affair of billiard tables. Men and women belonging to moderately 'advanced' sections of modern Western society find very few artificial obstacles in their path. Most of the conventions and taboos through which Octave and Armance had to force their way have crumbled out of existence. Their disappearance is due to a variety of causes, of which the decay of organized religion is perhaps the most important. The effects of disbelief have been reinforced by events which have occurred in spheres quite other than the religious. Thus, it is obvious that sexual morality would not have changed as radically as it has if the decay of religion had not synchronized with the perfection of a contraceptive technique which has robbed sexual indulgence of most of its terrors and, consequently, of much of its sinfulness. To take another case, increased prosperity has rendered self-denial less desperately necessary (and therefore less meritorious) than it was for the majority of men and women a few generations ago. Rationalization has led to over-production, and over-production calls insistently for a compensating over-consumption. Economic necessities easily and rapidly become moral virtues, and the first duty of the modern consumer is not to consume little, as in the pre-industrial epoch, but to consume much, to go on consuming more and more. Asceticism is bad citizenship, self-indulgence has become a social virtue. Let us consider now the effect on obstacle racing of recent changes in the organization of society. Modern societies are democracies stratified according to wealth. The hereditary principle has, to all intents, been abolished. There are no longer any divine rights, with the result that there are no longer any good manners; for good manners are the expression of the respect which is due to those who have a divine right to be respected. In an aristocratic society, like that in which Octave and Armance lived, every individual has divine rights entitling him to respect; each makes claims and each admits the justice of every one else's claims. Result—an exquisite politeness, elaborate codes of honour and etiquette. Aristocracy is dead; politeness and etiquette and the point of honour are but the shadows of themselves. Most of the obstacles with which the course of the well-bred racer was once so plentifully interrupted have consequently vanished. (Some of these obstacles, it should be remembered, were of the most alarming nature. For example, anger and impatience had to be kept under an iron restraint. To be short with a man was to risk being called out to fight a duel. Octave was severely wounded by, and himself murdered, a young man who wrote him an impertinent note.)

Smashing obstacles is fun, and the fun, being a blow for freedom, is meritorious; smashing, you make the best of both worlds. The first flat racers after a régime of obstacle racing have a splendid time. It is only when flat racing has become the rule and not the bold exception, that its flatness begins to pall. Luckily, this flattening process is slow. Obstacles are not destroyed simultaneously in all the strata of a society. Some classes may still be wildly steeple-chasing over taboos and across yawning gulfs of prohibition years after the rest of the world has taken to flat racing. Moreover, the phantoms of old obstacles long survive their death—in literature (for we continue to read old books), in the memories of ageing individuals. Smashing ghosts is at least the ghost of fun, the ghost of a meritorious blow for freedom. Contemporary England is full of heroic ghost-smashers. Not all, of course, of our obstacles are phantasmal; the course of most individual lives is dotted even to-day with solid barriers. The smashing of them will provide large numbers of people with amusement for a considerable time to come. There are many others, however, who are already finding the flat racing a bore. (The statement is sweeping and unverifiable; one can only rely on one's own observation and the evidence of contemporary fiction.) For most of these bored ones, it is true, habit has rendered a chronic 'good time' indispensably necessary. Confronted by an obstacle, whether external or internal, they suffer, genuinely. Which does not, however, prevent them from being bored when there is no obstacle and they are at liberty to run their race of gastronomic, sexual, and recreational indulgence unhindered and on the moral flat. '*Il n'est pas bon d'être trop libre. Il n'est pas bon d'avoir toutes les nécessités.*' Pascal was a realistic psychologist.

Suicide and a nunnery were the winning-posts towards which Octave and Armance crawled and scrambled. Unsatisfactory goals; but the race itself—that was never dull. (Incidentally, such winning-posts were not the inevitable or even the common conclusion of these bygone obstacle races. The suicide rate is far higher to-day than it was when Octave took his fatal dose of laudanum; madness and neurasthenia are much commoner.) The only complaint one could make against such a race as that which Stendhal describes is that it might prove to be too thrilling by half. For those who like a quiet life, its exaltations and agonies, its pains and raptures would be altogether too intense. But for those, and they are very many, who do *not* like a quiet life, how exceedingly satisfactory! Much more satisfactory, for example, than even the fastest flat racing. The pleasurable excitements to be derived from outwardly and inwardly permitted self-indulgence are insipid compared with those which are to be got from laboriously advancing (or even on occasion not advancing) over psychological obstacles towards a desired goal. No reasonable hedonist can consent to be a flat racer. Abolishing obstacles, he abolishes half his pleasures. And at the same time he abolishes most of his dignity as a human being. For the dignity of man consists precisely on his ability to restrain himself from dashing away along the flat, in his capacity to raise obstacles in his own path.

In the past man constructed most of these obstacles out of materials furnished by religion; and even when the obstacles were essentially economic, he took care to drape them picturesquely in religious or religious-ethical tapestries. The economic obstacles still exist; but for most men they are slightly, and for some much, lower than in the past. At the same time most of the religious obstacles, together with many of the ethical obstacles which it was reasonable for believing Christians to place in their own path, have collapsed. Modern man finds himself in the position of those Israelites who were called upon to make bricks without straw; he may desire to bar his way with obstacles a little more elaborate and subtle than those which laws and the current conventions pile clumsily across his path— he may desire to do this, I repeat, but he finds at hand no convenient raw materials out of which to manufacture such obstacles: nothing, that is to say, but what he can draw out of his own being. Yes, he must draw the materials for his obstacles entirely out of his own being, and he must find in the needs of his own being his sufficient reasons for setting up obstacles at all. He will take to obstacle racing, not because obstacle racing pleases God and flat racing does not, but because the having to climb over obstacles is in the last resort more pleasurable than trotting along on the flat and because the turning back from self-erected obstacles is, in many cases, the most nobly and dignifiedly human thing a man can do. Henceforth the only acceptable ethic will be an ethic based upon a verifiable psychology; morals, it seems, are destined to become a branch of medicine. If there are to be obstacles (and more or less often, more or less clearly, we are all conscious of a desire for obstacles), it is for science to decide what they shall be like, how constructed, where placed. And if the science is genuinely scientific, it will prescribe the setting up, here and there, of quite fantastic obstacles, it will deliberately queer the pitch of even the most legitimate and reasonable desires. 'Here,' it will say, 'you must plant an irrational prohibition, here a preposterous taboo, here a whole series of frankly anti-biological impediments.' Absurd; but then the human spirit *is* absurd, the whole process of living is utterly unreasonable. Absurdly enough, men, like obstacles, cannot be spiritually healthy without them, feel bored and ill when they take to flat racing. A realistic science can only accept the fact and prescribe accordingly.

In the past, obstacles were often gratuitously high, numerous, and neck-breaking. Inevitably; for if you set up obstacles, not for your own sake, but with the idea of pleasing a deity, it is obvious that they will tend to assume the super-human proportions of the being for whose sake they are created. Thought has a life of its own independent of its thinkers, and even, on occasion, hostile to it. A notion comes into existence and, obeying the laws of its notional being, proceeds to grow with all the irresistibleness and inevitability of a planted seed, or a crystal suspended in a saturated solution. For a growing notion, human minds are simply receptacles of crystal-forming liquid, simply seed beds more or less well manured. In the end the grown thought often comes to dominate its thinkers, to impose upon them a way of life which it is not to their advantage to adopt. Sometimes the growing thought is susceptible of direct embodiment. The history of machinery is a case in point. The germinal notion of machines has grown in the minds, and been progressively embodied by the hands, of successive craftsmen-thinkers, until now machinery is our master and we are compelled to live, not as we would like to live, but as it commands. The history of the next few centuries will be, among other things, the history of men's efforts to redomesticate the monster they have created, to reassert a human mastery over these bits of embodied thought at present so domineeringly rebellious.

The history of the notion of God is like that of the notion of machinery: once planted, it grew, it assumed an independent life of its own, and ended by imposing upon its cultivators (its 'hosts,' in the language of parasitology) a novel and at times disadvantageous mode of existence. But while the notion of machinery still goes on growing and embodying itself in ever new forms, the notion of God (of God, at any rate, as a personal being) has not only ceased to grow, but is even ceasing to live. The idea has been attacked at the root, with the result that all the vast superstructure of trunk, branches, and leaves has withered. One of the ramifications of this great religious tree was a morality of obstacles. God likes us to go in for obstacle racing, and the more impossibly, the more superhumanly difficult the obstacles, the better pleased He is. This was the religious theory. Its acceptance entailed, as I have said, a quite gratuitous trenching and barricading of the human race-course. It will be the business of science to discover a set of obstacles at least as excitingly and sportingly difficult as those which Octave and Armance had to surmount, but less dangerous to sanity and life, and, in spite of their absurdity, somehow compatible with an existence rationally organized for happiness and social progress. It remains to be seen how far, without the aid of a mythology, it will be successful.

TO THE PURITAN
ALL THINGS ARE IMPURE

MRS. GRUNDY resembles the King and that infernal worm of the Bible—she cannot die. *La Grundy est morte. Vive la Grundy!* There is no getting rid of her; she is immortal and succumbs only to be reborn. Disguised as Sir William Joynson-Hicks (for she frequently wears trousers), the old lady has been very active in England during the last few years. When the General Election put an end to Jix and his party, the optimists hoped that an end had been put to Mrs. Grundy. But the optimists, as usual, were wrong. In the sphere of sexual behaviour the new government is as rigidly orthodox as the old, and as actively intolerant. Among the last acts of the departing Home Secretary were the banning of D. H. Lawrence's novel, *Lady Chatterley's Lover*, and the confiscation of the registered letter containing the manuscript of his 'Pansies.' One of the first acts of his

Labourite successor was to set the police on to D. H. Lawrence's exhibition of paintings. *La Grundy est morte. Vive la Grundy!*

Sexual orthodoxy preserves not only its Athanasian Creed, but also its Grand Inquisitor. 'I believe in one heterosexual Love, monogamous and indissoluble. And I believe in Respectability. And above all in Silence.' Against the heretics who will not accept this profession of sexual faith, the Grand Inquisitors are permanently at war. At the beginning of last century, English Catholics and Jews had no political rights; atheists were expelled from English universities; blasphemers were severely punished. To-day a man is free to have any or no religion; about the Established Church and its divinities he can say almost anything he likes. But woe to him if he deviates from the narrow path of sexual orthodoxy! Penal servitude awaits those who act on their disbelief in the exclusive sanctity of heterosexuality; and for sexual blasphemy—that is to say, the writing of certain forbidden words and the frank description or representation of certain acts which every one performs—the penalty ranges from confiscation of the offending picture or writing to a fine and, possibly, in certain cases, imprisonment. It will thus be seen that, as things stand at present, any member of the Holy Trinity may be insulted with almost perfect impunity. But do, or say, or draw anything to offend Mrs. Grundy, and the avenging Inquisitor will immediately swoop down on you. Mrs. Grundy, in a word, is the only deity officially recognized by the English State. Men are free not to worship the God of Anglicanism; but the law compels them to bow down before the divine Grundy.

To argue the case against Grundyism would be easy, but wholly unprofitable. For in these matters, it is obvious, argument is perfectly useless. Argument appeals to reason, and there is no reason in Grundyism. There are at best only rationalizations of prejudices— prejudices that, in most individual Grundyites, date back to the teaching received in childhood. Those who accept the creed of sexual orthodoxy do so because, in Pavlov's phrase, their reflexes have been conditioned at an impressionable period. It would be absurd to doubt the sincerity of people like Mr. Sumner of the New York Vice Society, and the right honourable gentlemen who have filled the post of Home Secretary in England. They are obviously quite genuinely shocked by such things as *Lady Chatterley's Lover* and Lawrence's paintings. Such things *really* disgust and outrage them. Given their upbringing, it is inevitable; just as it is inevitable that Pavlov's dogs, after having been regularly fed to the sound of a bell, should start to dribble with hungry anticipation each time, in the future, that the bell is rung. Our vice-crusaders and Home Secretaries were doubtless brought up in surroundings where an improper word, an overfrank reference in Saxon phrases to the processes of reproduction and evacuation (notice how perfectly respectable these homely acts become when shrouded in the decent obscurity of a learned language!), was accompanied, not by anything so mild as the tinkling of a bell, but by appalling silences, by the blushing or swooning away of maiden aunts, by the sadly pious horror or Jehovahistic indignation of clergymen and schoolmasters. So that to this day they cannot hear these words or read these descriptions without at once recapturing (the process is as automatic as the salivation of Pavlov's dogs) the painful emotions aroused in them during childhood by the portentous accompaniments and consequences of what I have called sexual blasphemy. At present, most of those old enough to be occupying positions of power and responsibility were brought up in environments which conditioned their reflexes into the form of Grundyism. A time may come, perhaps, when these posts will be filled by men whose reflexes have not been so conditioned. When the contemporary child takes a normal, healthy interest in sex and scatology, the majority of young parents do not weep over him, or beat him, or tell him that his soul will roast in hell-fire. It follows, therefore, that his future reactions to sex will be less violently painful than the reactions of those who were children in the high old days of Podsnapian respectability. We are therefore justified in cherishing a mild hope for the future. For when I said that Mrs. Grundy was immortal, I was exaggerating. She may, old cat that she is, possess nine lives; but she is not everlasting. That a time may come when she will be, if not stone dead, at least enfeebled, chronically moribund, is, as we have seen, quite possible. Moreover, it is perfectly certain that during long periods of history she hardly existed at all. If we throw our eyes over the whole expanse of historical time, we perceive that active Grundyism is not a normal phenomenon. During the longest periods of recorded history puritanism has been, if not absolutely inexistent, at least without significance or power. The epochs of highest civilization have been conspicuously unpuritanical. It was to the naked Aphrodite that the Greeks of the fifth and sixth centuries B. C. made sacrifice, not to the much-petticoated divinity worshipped by the Pilgrim Fathers, by the later Podsnap and our contemporary vice-crusaders and Home Secretaries. Seen through the eyes of the philosophic historian, the Puritan reveals himself as the most abnormal sexual pervert of whom we have record, while Grundyism stands out as the supremely unnatural vice.

It was against this unnatural vice and the perverts who practise it that D. H. Lawrence waged almost his latest battle. A militant, crusading moralist, he hurled himself on what he regarded as the evil thing, the wicked people. But unfortunately the evil thing is sacred in our modern world, and the wicked people are precisely those Good Citizens who wield the powers of the State. Lawrence was often discomfited. The giant Grundy popped her huge crinoline over him and extinguished him by force. But not for long; his courage and his energy were inextinguishable and, in spite of the Home Secretaries, the bright dangerous flame of his art broke out again, the warning, denouncing, persuading voice was heard once more—up to the very end.

Cultured and tolerant people often ask: What is the point of this crusading? What is the point of shocking the Jixes into legal retaliation? What is the point of using the brief Saxon words that people shudder at, when you can express the same meaning, more or less, by means of circumlocutions and Graeco-Roman polysyllables? Might not Grundyism be attacked without ringing those particular alarm-bells which cause the mouths of the smut-hounds, not indeed to water, like those of Pavlov's dogs, but to foam with righteous indignation? In a word, might not as good or even better results be obtained if the crusade were conducted with tact and circumspection?

The answer to all these questions is: No. What Lawrence was crusading for was the admission by the conscious spirit of the right of the body and the instincts, not merely to a begrudged existence, but to an equal honour with itself. Man is an animal that thinks. To be a first-rate human being, a man must be both a first-rate animal and a first-rate thinker. (And, incidentally, he cannot be a first-rate thinker, at any rate about human affairs, unless he is also a first-rate animal.) From the time of Plato onwards there has been a tendency to exalt the thinking, spiritual man at the expense of the animal. Christianity confirmed Platonism; and now, in its turn, what I may call Fordism, or the philosophy of industrialism, confirms, though with important modifications, the spiritualizing doctrines of Christianity. Fordism demands that we should sacrifice the animal man (and along with the animal large portions of the thinking, spiritual man) not indeed to God, but to the Machine. There is no place in the factory, or in that larger factory which is the modern industrialized world, for animals on the one hand, or for artists, mystics, or even, finally, individuals on the other. Of all the ascetic religions Fordism is that which demands the cruellest mutilations of the human psyche—demands the cruellest mutilations and offers the smallest spiritual returns. Rigorously practised for a few generations, this dreadful religion of the machine will end by destroying the human race.

If humanity is to be saved there must be reforms, not merely in the social and economic spheres, but also within the individual psyche. Lawrence concerned himself primarily with these psychological reforms. The problem, for him, was to bring the animal and the thinker together again, was to make them co-operate in the building up of consummate manhood. In order to effect this bringing together certain barriers must be broken down. They are strong barriers; for the conscious mind has taken extraordinary precautions to keep itself out of contact with the body and its instincts. The spirit refuses to be livingly aware of the animal man. Very significant in this context are the tabooed words which describe in the directest possible manner the characteristic functions of bodily life. Early training has so conditioned the reflexes of the normal bourgeois and his wife that they shudder whenever one of these words is pronounced. For these words bring the mind into direct contact with the physical reality which it is so desperately anxious to ignore. The circumlocutions and the scientific polysyllables do not bring the mind into this direct contact. They are mere algebraical symbols, almost empty of living, physical significance—a fact which must somewhat diminish the hope for the future which I expressed just now. Brought up in a world that is learning to treat sexual matters only too scientifically, the future Jixes and Sumners will be quite undisturbed by literary references to micturition phantasies, autoerotism, and the like. But if the same phenomena are described in plain Saxon words, they will probably be just as painfully shocked as the present inquisitors. For when these Saxon words are pronounced the mind suddenly finds itself in actual touch with that physical reality which Platonism, Christianity, and Fordism have one after another insisted on its ignoring. It shrinks with horror. But it ought not to shrink with horror. Lawrence set out to overcome this shrinking. The methods he used were drastic—too drastic for many even of those who, in principle, were on his side. 'More tact, more circumspection!' they implored. But the use of forbidden words, the describing and portraying of things ordinarily veiled were absolutely essential tactics in the crusade. The mind had to be made conscious of the physical reality from which it was accustomed to shrink. This was the only way of doing it. The fact that people are shocked is the best proof that they need shocking. Their reflexes have been wrongly conditioned; they should be given a course of shocks until the conditioning is undone. The theory, I am sure, is psychologically sound. But to put it into practice is difficult. At every ringing of their familiar 'pornographic' bell, the right-thinkingly conditioned smuthounds foam at the mouth. And unfortunately they are in a position to do more than foam; they are in a position to open our letters, confiscate our books and burn our pictures. What's to be done about it? Perhaps Professor Pavlov might be able to tell us.

DOCUMENT

FROM the reports of a Debate on the censorship of obscene literature in the United States Senate, March 1930. Senator Smoot of Utah: 'I did not believe there were such books printed in the world.' (Senator Smoot had brought, as exhibits, Robert Burns's *Poems* (unexpurgated edition), Balzac's *Contes Drolatiques*, Casanova's *Memoirs*, George Moore's *Story Teller's Holiday*, D. H. Lawrence's *Lady Chatterley's Lover*, *My Life and Loves*, by Frank Harris, and that Mrs. Beeton's cookery book of love-making, the *Kama Sutra*.) 'They are lower than the beasts. . . . If I were a Customs Inspector, this obscene literature would only be admitted over my dead body. . . . I'd rather have a child of mine use opium than read these books.' (Compare with this the yet more heroic declaration of our own Mr. James Douglas. Mr. Douglas would rather give a child prussic acid than allow it to read *The Well of Loneliness*. In an article written at the time I offered to provide Mr. Douglas with a child, a bottle of prussic acid, a copy of *The Well of Loneliness*, and (if he kept his word and chose to administer the acid) a handsome memorial in marble to be erected wherever he might appoint, after his execution. The offer, I regret to say, was not accepted.)

Senator Blease of South Carolina was more eloquent even than Senator Smoot. True, he was not prepared to give children opium and prussic acid in preference to improper literature, but he was quite ready to 'see the democratic and republican form of government forever destroyed, if necessary to protect the virtue of the womanhood of America. . . . The virtue of one little sixteen-year-old girl is worth more to America than every book that ever came into it from any other country. . . . I love womanhood. Take from a government the purity of its womanhood and that government will be destroyed.'

POINTS OF VIEW

ANGELIN, Bishop of Belley, 'was wont to say: "I for my part can look indifferently upon any woman whatsoever; but I forthwith flay them all." Whereby he meant that he mentally withdrew their skin and contemplated the foul corruption that lurked within.'

Swift's celebrated remark about the woman he had seen flayed in a dissecting room belongs to the same family of ideas—a most respectable family, which can trace its descent at least as far back as Boethius. The Dean of St. Patrick's had a genuine Father of the Church in him. One side of him was own brother to that formidable Odo of Cluny, whose comments on the fair sex are so justly famous. The following translation emits but the faintest tinkling echo of those prodigious thunders of the Latin original. 'If men,' writes Odo, 'could see beneath the skin, as the lynxes of Boeotia are said to see into the inward parts, then the sight of a woman would be nauseous unto them. All that beauty consists but in phlegm and blood and humours and gall. If a man consider that which is hidden within the nose, the throat, and the belly, he will find filth everywhere; and if we cannot bring ourselves, even with the tips of our fingers, to touch such phlegm or dung, wherefore do we desire to embrace this bag of filth itself?'

Listen now to Michelet. I make no effort to render the almost hysterical lyricism of the original, but translate quite literally.

'An incomparable illustration from Coste and Gerbe's handbook' (Coste was a professor of embryology, Gerbe an anatomical draughtsman) 'shows the same organ (the matrix) under a less frightful aspect, which yet moves the beholder to tears. . . .

'Gerbe's few plates (for the most part unsigned)—this unique and astonishing atlas—are a temple of the future which, later on, in a better age, will fill all hearts with religion. One must fall on one's knees before daring to look at them.

'The great mystery of generation had never before appeared in art with all its charm, its true sanctity. I do not know the astonishing artist. I thank him none the less. Every man who has had a mother will thank him.

'He has given us the form, the colour, nay, much

more, he has given us the *morbidezza*, the tragic grace of these things, the profound emotion of them. Is it by dint of sheer accuracy? or did he feel all this? I know not, but such the effect is.

'Oh sanctuary of grace, made to purify all hearts, how many things you reveal to us!

'We learn, to begin with, that Nature, prodigal as she is of outward beauties, has placed the greatest within. The most thrilling are hidden, as though engulfed, in the depths of life itself.

'One learns, moreover, that love is something visible. The tenderness lavished upon us by our mothers, their dear caresses and the sweetness of their milk—all this can be recognized, felt, divined (and adored!) in this ineffable sanctuary of love and pain.'[1]

Well, well, well. . . .

---
[1] From Michelet's *L'Amour.*

ETHICS IN ANDALUSIA

Two newspapers are published at Granada, one Catholic, one liberal and anti-clerical. Their inky warfare rivals that of Mr. Potts and his detested colleague in *The Pickwick Papers*. A recent sojourn on the Moorish acropolis was pleasingly enlivened for me by the spectacle of the battle's daily vicissitudes. One skirmish in particular delighted me. It was over a play—one of those pleasant little farces which Spanish authors turn out with such facility and Spanish actors perform with such a lively brilliance. Produced at one of the local theatres, it had won from the critic of the liberal sheet unqualified praise—columns of it; for Spanish journalists of the second rank possess an almost unbelievable capacity for clothing the minimum of significance in the maximum of verbiage. I do not pretend that I read the article, for it was strictly unreadable; but I glanced at it for a sufficient number of seconds to know, not what it was about, for it was about nothing, but what was the sentiment that inspired it. Next day the clericals launched a counter-attack. They were not going to recommend immoral plays to their readers, not they. They left it to the liberals to commit such infamies. They had been disgusted, but not at all surprised, to see that the critic of their contemporary had so far pandered to immorality as to praise—I forget the name of the piece. For their own part, they had no hesitation in pronouncing it an infamous production. But if any of their readers wished to go to a moral play, they could recommend—— Here the name of the translation of an English crook play, which had just been put on at the other theatre. Needless to say, after reading this article I rushed to procure tickets for the farce. The reality, however, was bitterly disappointing. The infamy denounced so lyrically by the Fathers of the Church turned out to be the mildest little affair, such as French parents take their children to for a Christmas treat. There were a few jokes about the tender passion, a character who found the bonds of matrimony irksome; that was all. I came home feeling that I should like to sue the proprietors of the clerical paper for the price of my ticket. What swindlers! And it occurred to me that perhaps all the great scourgers of past immoralities were perhaps as fraudulent, in their loud denunciations, as the very right-thinking journalist who warned the Granadines against the corrupting influence of an ingenuous little farce. Suppose some time-machine could transport us back into the world described so glowingly and with such obvious gusto by Juvenal; or into that, at the very end of the imperial epoch, denounced with so much Christian zeal (and for the ungodly, so alluringly!) by Salvianus: I have a strong suspicion that we should be sadly disappointed. What, only this? And we should immediately take our return ticket to twentieth-century Paris or New York. For the truth is that, if you speak about it in the appropriate language, practically any act can be made to seem practically anything, from saintly to infamous. Read George Sand, and you will be convinced that the best, the infallible way to please one's Creator is to satisfy one's amorous caprices, even if they should be focussed on the footman. Read, shall we say, Charles Maurras's comments on George Sand, and you will be made to feel that the lover of Musset and Chopin was an insatiable man-eater, and that her doctrines were both silly and profoundly immoral. It is entirely a question of language. If you have strong moral feelings (or else no moral feelings, but merely malice, merely a desire to show off) and a talent for using intemperate language in an effective manner, you can make people believe that the world is fairly bristling with the most appalling iniquities. For those who have the right sort of literary or oratorical talent, taking the high moral line is one of the most paying of professions. Even in Granada. For, as I have said, the lash was unsparingly applied by the clerical critic. When he had done with it, the poor little farce might have been, at the least, Lord Rochester's *Sodom*. His review, I am sure, must have doubled the box office receipts.

Looked at dispassionately and with Martian eyes, perhaps the oddest thing of all was the fact that the right-thinking critic who had denounced the farce should have proceeded to recommend, as eminently moral, the crook play. The farce, it is true, dealt with adultery, which is one of the manifestations of the deadly sin of lust. But the crook play dealt with murder and robbery, which are manifestations of the equally deadly sins of anger and avarice. Moreover, the murder and the robbery were done, in spite of the rules of classic art, *coram populo*, on the stage, whereas the adultery took place, discreetly, off. What is more, one at least of the crooks was decidedly a sympathetic character, whom any suggestible and hero-worshipping young person might almost justifiably desire to resemble. It will thus be seen that the right-thinking critic was recommending as moral a play in which two deadly sins were painted with extreme vividness and in attractive colours, while he denounced as infamous the much less vivid representation of another deadly sin. The judgment of the right-thinking critic of Granada would undoubtedly be approved by right-thinking critics in all other parts of the world. It is highly significant, in this context, that the word 'immoral' should have acquired among the English-speaking peoples a specialized and technical meaning. When we say of a millionaire that he is a very 'immoral' man, we are not referring to his vulture-like rapacity, his avarice, his swinish gluttony, his vanity and cruelty; we are referring exclusively to his habit of pinching the fleshier parts of his typists' anatomies and taking chorus-girls out to supper. Similarly, an 'immoral' book is one which deals with acts—it may be, perfectly licit and conjugal acts—of a sexual nature. An 'immoral' picture is a nude, not necessarily even in a specifically amorous posture; in England, at least, a nude is, legally speaking, immoral if it has not been freed from its superfluous hair. What censors cut out of films is never the shooting, the burglary, the profitable swindling and gambling; it is the kisses.

What justifies the right-thinking attitude is the fact (in my opinion enormously creditable to human nature) that the deadly sin of concupiscence is, for most people, much more attractive than the deadly sins of anger and even avarice. Granted the preliminary assumption that concupiscence is wicked, right-thinkers are justified in specially discriminating against the representations of this sin. For such representations are likely to lead more people into sexual crime than would be led into crimes of violence by the representations of murder and robbery.

Among the right-thinking the doctrine of the inherent wickedness of concupiscence is still held with an extraordinary intensity. Parnell was ruined because the Nonconformist supporters of Irish Home Rule were shocked by his adultery; the possibility of his being implicated in the campaigns of murder had left them relatively unmoved. In the famous Thompson-Bywaters murder case we were shown the spectacle of a woman passionately in love, but so respectable and embedded in such an intensely respectable stratum of society, that she preferred murdering her husband to going and living in open sin with her lover. Bywaters and Mrs. Thompson were hanged—pathetic martyrs to a system of ethics which assigns the palm of immorality to the sin of concupiscence. A more recent example will serve to confirm my thesis. Some few days after leaving Granada, I picked up a copy of the Paris edition of the Chicago *Tribune*, belatedly arrived in Andalusia, and read that some unfortunate person in California had been condemned to fifty years' imprisonment for assaulting a young lady. Now, people who assault young ladies are obviously intolerable nuisances, and should be firmly dealt with; but when it comes to fifty years' imprisonment—well, really, isn't that carrying firmness a little too far? My own idea of a suitable punishment for masculine assaulters would be to subject them in their turn to the assault of a dozen or two of sturdy and active females. In his fascinating book on *The Sexual Life of Savages* (so infinitely more sensibly, hygienically, and morally arranged than the sexual life of ladies and gentlemen), Professor Malinowski describes the treatment to which masculine trespassers are subjected by the women of certain tribes of Trobriand Islanders. I will not go into details; suffice it to say that the methods of the Trobriand ladies are exceedingly drastic. My suggestion is that these methods should be used, by a picked band of female executioners, on all men found guilty of assault on a member of the opposite sex. It seems to me very doubtful whether any man once punished in this way would ever offend again. But professional justice is not poetical—that is to say, not sensible; punishments do not fit crimes. The assaulters get sent to gaol—in California, for half a century at a time. A sentence of such enormity is only possible in a society where the word 'immoral' has come to connote, almost exclusively, acts of a sexual nature. The incorrect sexual act corresponds, in certain contemporary societies, to the expression of heretical opinions in Catholic and early Protestant Europe during the ages of faith.

There are indications that the scale of values in our ethical system is now undergoing a gradual modification. In large sections of contemporary society the importance of sexual acts has been minimized—unduly, even. At the same time, the dislike of cruelty seems to be steadily growing, and also (which is pregnant with the most important consequences) a certain tenderness of conscience with regard to the manifestations of avarice and the love of money is beginning to be noticeable. The mediaeval Catholic Church professed a passionate hatred for the love of money and used all the weapons in both its spiritual and temporal armouries to prevent men from indulging too freely in this sin. Under Calvin and the later Protestants the Christian attitude towards money underwent a great change. The Old Testament notion, that prosperity was a sign of virtue (which indeed it is, if you limit virtue to prudence, industry, thrift, and the like), was revived. Today, under the influence of Socialists, Tolstoyans, William-Morrisites, and the various other modern protestants against industrialism, a certain reaction towards the mediaeval standards of economic morality has begun to set in. The time, it may be, is not so very far distant when the most hateful heresies, in the eyes of all right-thinking people, will be, not amorous, but economic heresies; when fifty years behind the bars will be the fate of the over-monied rather than of the over-sexed. Whether this stage of things will be preferable to the existent state I cannot say; it will be different, that is all one can be certain of. It is fashionable nowadays to call every change a progress. I myself prefer the older, the less presumptuous and self-congratulatory name.

SECTION IV

FOREHEADS VILLAINOUS LOW

In *A Farewell to Arms*, Mr. Ernest Hemingway ventures, once, to name an Old Master. There is a phrase, quite admirably expressive (for Mr. Hemingway is a most subtle and sensitive writer), a single phrase, no more, about 'the bitter nail-holes' of Mantegna's Christs; then quickly, quickly, appalled by his own temerity, the author passes on (as Mrs. Gaskell might hastily have passed on, if she had somehow been betrayed into mentioning a water-closet), passes on shamefacedly to speak once more of Lower Things.

There was a time, not so long ago, when the stupid and uneducated aspired to be thought intelligent and cultured. The current of aspiration has changed its direction. It is not at all uncommon now to find intelligent and cultured people doing their best to feign stupidity and to conceal the fact that they have received an education. Twenty years ago it was still a compliment to say of a man that he was clever, cultivated, interested in the things of the mind. To-day 'highbrow' is a term of contemptuous abuse. The fact is surely significant.

In decent Anglo-Saxon society one may not be a highbrow. What may one be, then? Or rather, since the categorical imperatives of snobbery and convention are involved, what *must* one be? In America one must be, loudly and heartily and bibulously, the Good Mixer. Your refined Englishman deplores the loudness and heartiness; good mixing in the Old Country must be done in a superiorly genteel and Public-Schooly fashion. The ideal Englishman and Englishwoman are those two delightful young married people, who are the permanent hero and heroine of all the friendly jokes in *Punch*. They have about a thousand a year and perhaps two children, who are perpetually making the sweetest, the most killingly Barrieesque remarks. They are, of course, the greatest dears and awfully good sports; and as for their sense of humour—it's really priceless. When they find a couple of woodlice in their garden, they instantly christen them Agatha and Archibald—than which, as every one will agree, nothing could well be funnier. Indeed, their sense of humour is so constantly in evidence, that one would be almost tempted to believe that they take nothing seriously. But one would be wrong. These charming jesters have hall-marked hearts and all the right, all the genuinely upper-middle-class instincts about everything and everybody, including the highbrows, for whom they have a healthily Public-School contempt—mingled, however, with a certain secret and uncomfortable fear.

Dear priceless creatures! Of such is the kingdom of our anglican heaven. 'Go thou and do likewise,' commands the categorical imperative. I do my best to conform; but when the priceless ones draw near, I find myself obeying only the first part of the commandment; I *go*—as fast as I possibly can.

To what do we owe these two characteristically and, I would say, uniquely modern snobberies—the snobbery of stupidity and the snobbery of ignorance? What is it that makes so many of our contemporaries so anxious to be considered low-brows? I have often wondered. Here, for what they are worth, are the conclusions to which these speculations have led me.

Stupidity-snobbery and ignorance-snobbery are the fruits of universal education. Hence—for there can be no fruits without trees—their very recent appearance. The tree of universal education was only planted fifty years ago. It is now just beginning to bear.

Under the old dispensation, some people who might

have profited by education, remained uneducated; others, incapable of getting much out of an elaborate schooling, were nevertheless (thanks to the accident of their birth) elaborately schooled. On the whole, however, those who could profit by education generally got educated. For those who can profit by education develop as a rule—some in childhood, some in adolescence—an intense desire to be educated. When a desire is intense enough, it generally gets itself fulfilled. The educated class in mediaeval times probably contained a fair proportion of the profitably educable individuals (at any rate of the male sex) distributed throughout the population. The merit of a system of universal education is that it gives all profitably educable individuals a chance of receiving the schooling by which they, and through them perhaps also society, will profit. At the same time, however, it enormously increases the number of those who cannot profit much by education, but who nevertheless are more or less elaborately schooled.

When culture was confined to the few, it had a rarity-value comparable to that of pearls or caviar. The golden ages of culture-snobbery were the dark ages of education. When finally the Many were given the education which, when it was confined to the Few, had seemed so precious, so magically efficacious, they found out very quickly that the gift was not worth quite so much as they had supposed—that, in fact, there was nothing in it. And indeed, for the great majority of men and women, there obviously *is* nothing in culture. Nothing at all—neither spiritual satisfactions, nor social rewards. There are no spiritual satisfactions, because most people (perhaps fortunately) are not endowed with the curious mentality of those who can wring pleasure out of the abstractions and inactualities of a liberal education. And there are no social rewards, because, in a world where every one is educated, the mere fact of having been to school ceases automatically to be the key to success. Under a system of universal education, social rewards will tend to go only to those who have talent as well as schooling. The schooled but untalented Many find themselves just as badly off as they were before.

Professional democrats continue to prescribe education and yet more education as a remedy for every individual and social ill. For these people, it would seem, education is more than a simple medicine; it is a kind of magical elixir. Man has only to drink enough of it to be transformed into something superhuman.

'Ladies and gentlemen,' the quack earnestly begins. The people listen, rather apathetically; they have heard this sort of thing before. But when the benefactor of humanity hands out yet another bottle of his concoction, they accept it, they take their dose and hopefully wait for the effects. There are, as usual, no effects. Somebody starts to laugh. 'There's nothing in it,' says a rather vulgar voice. Indignantly, the benefactor of humanity produces authentic testimonials from John Stuart Mill, Francis Bacon, and St. Thomas Aquinas. In vain. The crowd doesn't believe in them. Why should it? It has had personal experience of the inefficacy of the elixir. 'There's nothing in it,' repeats the vulgar and resentful voice. The snobberies of stupidity and ignorance have come into being.

Universal education is still in its infancy; but the fruits of that young tree—oh, how astonishingly large they are already! The rapidity of their growth will surprise us less, however, when we remember with what loving care they have been fostered. Education brought them forth; but to Industry belongs the credit of their conscious and intelligent nurture.

If by some miracle the dreams of the educationists were realized and the majority of human beings began to take an exclusive interest in the things of the mind, the whole industrial system would instantly collapse. Given modern machinery, there can be no industrial prosperity without mass production. Mass production is impossible without mass consumption. Other things being equal, consumption varies inversely with the intensity of mental life. A man who is exclusively interested in the things of the mind will be quite happy (in Pascal's phrase) sitting quietly in a room. A man who has no interest in the things of the mind will be bored to death if he has to sit quietly in a room. Lacking thoughts with which to distract himself, he must acquire things to take their place; incapable of mental travel, he must move about in the body. In a word, he is the ideal consumer, the mass consumer of objects and of transport.

Now, it is obviously in the interests of industrial producers to encourage the good consumer and to discourage the bad. This they do by means of advertisement and of that enormous newspaper propaganda which always gratefully follows advertisement. Those who sit quietly in rooms with nothing but their thoughts and perhaps a book to amuse them, are represented as miserable, ridiculous, and even rather immoral. Happiness is a product of noise, company, motion, and the possession of objects. The more noise you listen to, the more people you have round you, the faster you move and the more objects you possess, the happier you will be—the happier and also the more normal and virtuous. In the modern industrial state, highbrows, being poor consumers, are bad citizens. Long live stupidity and ignorance!

Fostered by the propaganda of the industrialists, the fruits of universal education have sprouted and swollen out, like cabbages in the unsetting sunshine of an arctic summer. The new snobberies of stupidity and ignorance are now strong enough to wage war at least on equal terms with the old culture-snobbery. For still, an absurd anachronism, the dear old culture-snobbery bravely survives. Will it go down before its enemies? And, much more important, will the culture it so heroically and ridiculously stands up for, also go down? I hope, I even venture to think, it will not. There will always be a few people for whom the things of the mind are so vitally important that they will not, they simply cannot allow them to be overwhelmed.

'But will there always be such people?' questions an ironical demon. 'And what about the yearly increase in the numbers of the mentally deficient? And what about R. A. Fisher's demonstration of the way in which a society that measures success in economic terms must fatally and inevitably eliminate all heritable ability above the normal?'

Let us ignore the demon; or rather let us piously hope that something may be done about him before it is too late. In the meantime the battle between the rival snobberies comically rages. A sham fight still; there is as yet no actual persecution of highbrows. We are safe. But even as things are, there are wholesale desertions and betrayals. Caliban's mere contempt is enough to shame hundreds of highbrows into a denial of their nature and upbringing.

'You're cultured.' Caliban points accusingly. 'You're intelligent.'

'But no! How can you say such a thing?'

'I distinctly heard the word "Mantegna."'

'Impossible!'

'I did hear it.' Caliban is inexorable.

The highbrows shake their heads. 'Then it must have been a slip of the tongue. What we meant to say was "gin."'

THE NEW ROMANTICISM

The Romantics have come in for a great deal of varied abuse. The classicists have reproached them for their hysterical extravagance. The realists have called them liars and cowards who are afraid of the unpleasant truth. Moralists have disapproved of their exaltation of passion and emotion. Philosophers have complained of their prejudice against reason and their appeal to a facile mysticism. Socialists and believers in authority have disliked their individualism. Each enemy throws a different brickbat. But brickbats can be flung back. The Romantics can retort on the classicists that they are dull and rationally cold; on the realists that they are exclusively preoccupied with muck and lucre; on the moralists that their ideal of mere repression is stupid, because always unsuccessful; on the philosophers that their famous Pure Reason has taken them no nearer to the solution of the cosmic riddle than a cow's Pure Instinct; and on the authoritarians and socialists that their state tyranny and collectivism are at least as unnatural as limitless individualism. Pots and kettles may quarrel; but their colour is proverbially much the same. Most of the enemies of romanticism are, in their own way, as extravagant and one-sided (that is to say, as romantic) as the Romantics themselves.

The activities of our age are uncertain and multifarious. No single literary, artistic, or philosophic tendency predominates. There is a babel of notions and conflicting theories. But in the midst of this general confusion, it is possible to recognize one curious and significant melody, repeated in different keys and by different instruments in every one of the subsidiary babels. It is the tune of our modern romanticism.

It will be protested at once that no age could be less like that of the genuine Romantics than ours. And with this objection I make all haste to agree. The modern romanticism is not in the least like the romanticism of Moore and de Musset and Chopin, to say nothing of the romanticism of Shelley, of Victor Hugo, of Beethoven. In fact, it is the exact opposite of theirs. Modern romanticism is the old romanticism turned inside out, with all its values reversed. Their plus is the modern minus; the modern good is the old bad. What then was black is now white, what was white is now black. Our romanticism is the photographic negative of that which flourished during the corresponding years of last century.

It is in the sphere of politics that the difference between the two romanticisms is most immediately apparent. The revolutionaries of a hundred years ago were democrats and individualists. For them the supreme political value was that personal liberty, which Mussolini has described as a putrefying corpse and which the Bolsheviks deride as an ideal invented by and for the leisured bourgeoisie. The men who agitated for the English Reform Bill of 1832, who engineered the Parisian revolution of 1830, were liberals. Individualism and freedom were the ultimate goods which they pursued. The aim of the Communist Revolution in Russia was to deprive the individual of every right, every vestige of personal liberty (including the liberty of thought and the right to possess a soul), and to transform him into a component cell of the great 'Collective Man'—that single mechanical monster who, in the Bolshevik millennium, is to take the place of the unregimented hordes of 'soul-encumbered' individuals who now inhabit the earth. To the Bolshevik, there is something hideous and unseemly about the spectacle of anything so 'chaotically vital,' so 'mystically organic' as an individual with a soul, with personal tastes, with special talents. Individuals must be organized out of existence; the communist state requires, not men, but cogs and ratchets in the huge 'collective mechanism.' To the Bolshevik idealist, Utopia is indistinguishable from one of Mr. Henry Ford's factories. It is not enough, in their eyes, that men should spend only eight hours a day under the workshop discipline. Life outside the factory must be exactly like life inside. Leisure must be as highly organized as toil. Into the Christian Kingdom of Heaven men may only enter if they have become like little children. The condition of their entry into the Bolsheviks' Earthly Paradise is that they shall have become like machines.

Lest it be imagined that I have caricatured the communist doctrine, let me refer my readers to the numerous original documents quoted by Herr Fulop-Miller in his very interesting book on the cultural life of Soviet Russia, *The Mind and Face of Bolshevism*. They show clearly enough that the political doctrines elaborated by Lenin and his followers are the exact antithesis of the revolutionary liberalism preached by Godwin and dithyrambically chanted by Shelley a hundred years ago. Godwin and Shelley believed in pure individualism. The Bolsheviks believe in pure collectivism. One belief is as extravagantly romantic as the other. Men cannot live apart from society and without organization. But, equally, they cannot live without a certain modicum of privacy and personal liberty. The exclusive idealism of Shelley denies the obvious facts of human biology and economics. The exclusive materialism of Lenin denies the no less obvious and primary facts of men's immediate spiritual experiences. The revolutionary liberals were romantic in their refusal to admit that man was a social animal as well as an individual soul. The Bolshevists are romantic in denying that man is anything more than a social animal, susceptible of being transformed by proper training into a perfect machine. Both are extravagant and one-sided.

Modern romanticism is by no means confined to Russia or to politics. It has filtered into the thought and arts of every country. Communism has not imposed itself anywhere outside the boundaries of Russia; but the Bolsheviks' romantic disparagement of spiritual and individual values has affected, to a greater or less extent, the 'young' art and literature of every Western people. Thus, the whole 'Cubist' tendency in modern art (from which, one is grateful to notice, painters and sculptors seem to be in fairly general reaction) is deeply symptomatic of that revolt against the soul and the individual, to which the Bolsheviks have given practical and political, as well as artistic, expression. The Cubists deliberately eliminated from their art all that is 'mystically organic,' replacing it by solid geometry. They were the enemies of all 'sentimentality' (a favourite word in the Bolsheviks' vocabulary of insult), of all mere literature—that is to say, of all the spiritual and individual values which give significance to individual life. Art, they proclaimed, is a question of pure form. A Cubist picture is one from which everything that might appeal to the individual soul, as a soul, has been omitted. It is addressed exclusively (and addressed very often, let us admit, with consummate skill) to an abstract Aesthetic Man, who stands in much the same relation to the real complex human being as does the Economic Man of the socialists, or the mechanized component of the Bolsheviks' Collective Man.

The Cubist dehumanization of art is frequently accompanied by a romantic and sentimental admiration for machines. Fragments of machinery are generously scattered through modern painting. There are sculptors, who laboriously try to reproduce the forms invented by engineers. The ambition of advanced architects is to make dwelling-houses indistinguishable from factories; in Le Corbusier's phrase, a house is a 'machine for living in.'

'Young' writers are as fond of machinery as 'young'

artists. What dithyrambs in praise of machinery have issued, in free verse, from the Middle West of America! On the continent of Europe advanced writers have invented for their own delectation entirely fabulous Chicagos and New Yorks, where every house is a skyscraper and every skyscraper a factory full of incessantly turning wheels; where there are elevated railways in every street, aëroplanes circling round every chimney-pot, electric sky-signs on every blank wall, motor cars never doing less than sixty miles an hour, and a noise like seventy pandemoniums. Here is a translation of Maiakovski's lines on Chicago:—

> *Chicago: City*
> *Built upon a screw!*
> *Electro-dynamo-mechanical city!*
> *Spiral shaped—*
> *On a steel disk—*
> *At every stroke of the hour*
> *Turning itself round!*
> *Five thousand skyscrapers—*
> *Granite suns!*
> *The Squares—*
> *Mile-high, they gallop to heaven,*
> *Crawling with millions of men,*
> *Woven of steel hawsers,*
> *Flying Broadways. . . .*

Tom Moore's descriptions of the Orient in *Lalla Rookh* are far less fantastically romantic than this. The passion for machines, so characteristic of modern art, is a kind of regression to what I may call second boyhood. At twelve we were all mad about locomotives, ships' engines, machine tools. It was the ambition of every one of us to be a stoker, or an engine-driver—anything, provided only that our job should entail hourly contact with the adored machine. But growing up, most of us found that human souls are really more odd and interesting even than the most elaborate mechanism. The modern artist seems to have grown down; he has reverted to the preoccupations of his childhood. He is trying to be a primitive. So, it may be remembered, was the romantic Rousseau. But whereas Rousseau's savage was noble, refined, and intelligent, the primitive our modern artists would like to resemble is a mixture between the apache of the slums, the African negro, and the fifteen-year-old schoolboy. Our modern Rousseaus are contemptuous of psychology (how violently Proust was attacked by all the really advanced young people in Paris!); they deride metaphysics in any form; they despise reason and order, and though, illogically, they continue to write and paint, they regard all art as a waste of time. The ideal life, in their eyes, is one in which there is plenty of sport, noise, machinery, and sociable agitation.

Personally, I have no great liking for either of the romanticisms. If it were absolutely necessary for me to choose between them, I think I would choose the older one. An exaggeration of the significance of the soul and the individual, at the expense of matter, society, machinery, and organization, seems to me an exaggeration in the right direction. The new romanticism, so far as I can see, is headed straight towards death. (But then, what I call death, the new romantics would call life, and *vice versa.*) No, if I had my way, I would not choose either of the romanticisms; I would vote for the adoption of a middle course between them. The only philosophy of life which has any prospect of being permanently valuable is a philosophy which takes in all the facts—the facts of mind *and* the facts of matter, of instinct and intellect, of individualism *and* of sociableness. The wise man will avoid both extremes of romanticism and choose the realistic golden mean.

SELECTED SNOBBERIES

ALL men are snobs about something. One is almost tempted to add: There is nothing about which men cannot feel snobbish. But this would doubtless be an exaggeration. There are certain disfiguring and mortal diseases, about which there has probably never been any snobbery. I cannot imagine, for example, that there are any leprosy-snobs. More picturesque diseases, even when they are dangerous, and less dangerous diseases, particularly when they are the diseases of the rich, can be and very frequently are a source of snobbish self-importance. I have met several adolescent consumption-snobs, who thought that it would be romantic to fade away in the flower of youth, like Keats or Marie Bashkirtseff. Alas, the final stages of the consumptive fading are generally a good deal less romantic than these ingenuous young tubercle-snobs seem to imagine. To any one who has actually witnessed these final stages, the complacent poeticizings of these adolescents must seem as exasperating as they are profoundly pathetic. In the case of those commoner disease-snobs, whose claim to distinction is that they suffer from one of the maladies of the rich, exasperation is not tempered by very much sympathy. People who possess sufficient leisure, sufficient wealth, not to mention sufficient health, to go travelling from spa to spa, from doctor to fashionable doctor, in search of cures from problematical diseases (which, in so far as they exist at all, probably have their source in overeating) cannot expect us to be very lavish in our solicitude and pity.

Disease-snobbery is only one out of a great multitude of snobberies, of which now some, now others take pride of place in general esteem. For snobberies ebb and flow; their empire rises, declines, and falls in the most approved historical manner. What were good snobberies a hundred years ago are now out of fashion. Thus, the snobbery of family is everywhere on the decline. The snobbery of culture, still strong, has now to wrestle with an organized and active low-browism, with a snobbery of ignorance and stupidity unique, so far as I know, in the whole of history. Hardly less characteristic of our age is that repulsive booze-snobbery, born of American Prohibition. The malefic influences of this snobbery are rapidly spreading all over the world. Even in France, where the existence of so many varieties of delicious wine has hitherto imposed a judicious connoisseurship and has led to the branding of mere drinking as a brutish solecism, even in France the American booze-snobbery, with its odious accompaniments—a taste for hard drinks in general and for cocktails in particular—is making headway among the rich. Booze-snobbery has now made it socially permissible, and in some circles even rather creditable, for well-brought-up men and (this is the novelty) well-brought-up women of all ages, from fifteen to seventy, to be seen drunk, if not in public, at least in the very much tempered privacy of a party.

Modernity-snobbery, though not exclusive to our age, has come to assume an unprecedented importance. The reasons for this are simple and of a strictly economic character. Thanks to modern machinery, production is outrunning consumption. Organized waste among consumers is the first condition of our industrial prosperity. The sooner a consumer throws away the object he has bought and buys another, the better for the producer. At the same time, of course, the producer must do his bit by producing nothing but the most perishable articles. 'The man who builds a skyscraper to last for more than forty years is a traitor to the building trade.' The words are those of a great American contractor. Substitute motor car, boot, suit of clothes, etc., for skyscraper, and one year, three months, six months, and so on for forty years, and you have the gospel of any leader of any modern industry. The modernity-snob, it is obvious, is this industrialist's best friend. For modernity-snobs naturally tend to throw away their old possessions and buy new ones at a greater rate than those who are not modernity-snobs. Therefore it is in the producer's interest to encourage modernity-snobbery. Which in fact he does do—on an enormous scale and to the tune of millions and millions a year—by means of advertising. The newspapers do their best to help those who help them; and to the flood of advertisement is added a flood of less directly paid-for propaganda in favour of modernity-snobbery. The public is taught that up-to-dateness is one of the first duties of man. Docile, it accepts the reiterated suggestion. We are all modernity-snobs now.

Most of us are also art-snobs. There are two varieties of art-snobbery—the platonic and the unplatonic. Platonic art-snobs merely 'take an interest' in art. Unplatonic art-snobs go further and actually buy art. Platonic art-snobbery is a branch of culture-snobbery. Unplatonic art-snobbery is a hybrid or mule; for it is simultaneously a sub-species of culture-snobbery and of possession-snobbery. A collection of works of art is a collection of culture-symbols, and culture-symbols still carry social prestige. It is also a collection of wealth-symbols. For an art collection can represent money more effectively than a whole fleet of motor cars.

The value of art-snobbery to living artists is considerable. True, most art-snobs collect only the works of the dead; for an Old Master is both a safer investment and a holier culture-symbol than a living master. But some art-snobs are also modernity-snobs. There are enough of them, with the few eccentrics who like works of art for their own sake, to provide living artists with the means of subsistence.

The value of snobbery in general, its humanistic 'point,' consists in its power to stimulate activity. A society with plenty of snobberies is like a dog with plenty of fleas: it is not likely to become comatose. Every snobbery demands of its devotees unceasing efforts, a succession of sacrifices. The society-snob must be perpetually lion-hunting; the modernity-snob can never rest from trying to be up-to-date. Swiss doctors and the Best that has been thought or said must be the daily and nightly preoccupation of all the snobs respectively of disease and culture.

If we regard activity as being in itself a good, then we must count all snobberies as good; for all provoke activity. If, with the Buddhists, we regard all activity in this world of illusion as bad, then we shall condemn all snobberies out of hand. Most of us, I suppose, take up our position somewhere between the two extremes. We regard some activities as good, others as indifferent or downright bad. Our approval will be given only to such snobberies as excite what we regard as the better activities; the others we shall either tolerate or detest. For example, most professional intellectuals will approve of culture-snobbery (even while intensely disliking most individual culture-snobs), because it compels the philistines to pay at least some slight tribute to the things of the mind and so helps to make the world less dangerously unsafe for ideas than it otherwise might have been. A manufacturer of motor cars, on the other hand, will rank the snobbery of possessions above culture-snobbery; he will do his best to persuade people that those who have fewer possessions, particularly possessions on four wheels, are inferior to those who have more possessions. And so on. Each hierarchy culminates in its own particular Pope.

THE BEAUTY INDUSTRY

THE one American industry unaffected by the general depression of trade is the beauty industry. American women continue to spend on their faces and bodies as much as they spent before the coming of the slump—about three million pounds a week. These facts and figures are 'official,' and can be accepted as being substantially true. Reading them, I was only surprised by the comparative smallness of the sums expended. From the prodigious number of advertisements of aids to beauty contained in the American magazines, I had imagined that the personal appearance business must stand high up among the champions of American industry—the equal, or only just less than the equal, of bootlegging and racketeering, movies and automobiles. Still, one hundred and fifty-six million pounds a year is a tidy sum. Rather more than twice the revenue of India, if I remember rightly.

I do not know what the European figures are. Much smaller, undoubtedly. Europe is poor, and a face can cost as much in upkeep as a Rolls-Royce. The most that the majority of European women can do is just to wash and hope for the best. Perhaps the soap will produce its loudly advertised effects; perhaps it will transform them into the likeness of those ravishing creatures who smile so rosily and creamily, so peachily and pearlily, from every hoarding. Perhaps, on the other hand, it may not. In any case, the more costly experiments in beautification are still as much beyond most European means as are high-powered motor cars and electric refrigerators. Even in Europe, however, much more is now spent on beauty than was ever spent in the past. Not quite so much more as in America, that is all. But, everywhere, the increase has been undoubtedly enormous.

The fact is significant. To what is it due? In part, I suppose, to a general increase in prosperity. The rich have always cultivated their personal appearance. The diffusion of wealth—such as it is—now permits those of the poor who are less badly off than their fathers to do the same.

But this is, clearly, not the whole story. The modern

cult of beauty is not exclusively a function (in the mathematical sense) of wealth. If it were, then the personal appearance industries would have been as hardly hit by the trade depression as any other business. But, as we have seen, they have not suffered. Women are retrenching on other things than their faces. The cult of beauty must therefore be symptomatic of changes that have taken place outside the economic sphere. Of what changes? Of the changes, I suggest, in the status of women; of the changes in our attitude towards 'the merely physical.'

Women, it is obvious, are freer than in the past. Freer not only to perform the generally unenviable social functions hitherto reserved to the male, but also freer to exercise the more pleasing, feminine privilege of being attractive. They have the right, if not to *be* less virtuous than their grandmothers, at any rate to *look* less virtuous. The British Matron, not long since a creature of austere and even terrifying aspect, now does her best to achieve and perennially preserve the appearance of what her predecessor would have described as a Lost Woman. She often succeeds. But we are not shocked—at any rate, not morally shocked. Aesthetically shocked—yes; we may sometimes be that. But morally, no. We concede that the Matron is morally justified in being preoccupied with her personal appearance. This concession depends on another of a more general nature—a concession to the Body, with a large B, to the Manichæan principle of evil. For we have now come to admit that the body has its rights. And not only rights—duties, actually duties. It has, for example, a duty to do the best it can for itself in the way of strength and beauty. Christian-ascetic ideas no longer trouble us. We demand justice for the body as well as for the soul. Hence, among other things, the fortunes made by face-cream manufacturers and beauty-specialists, by the vendors of rubber reducing-belts and massage machines, by the patentees of hair-lotions and the authors of books on the culture of the abdomen.

What are the practical results of this modern cult of beauty? The exercises and the massage, the health-motors and the skin-foods—to what have they led? Are women more beautiful than they were? Do they get something for the enormous expenditure of energy, time, and money demanded of them by the beauty-cult? These are questions which it is difficult to answer. For the facts seem to contradict themselves. The campaign for more physical beauty seems to be both a tremendous success and a lamentable failure. It depends how you look at the results.

It is a success in so far as more women retain their youthful appearance to a greater age than in the past.

THE BEAUTY INDUSTRY

'Old ladies' are already becoming rare. In a few years, we may well believe, they will be extinct. White hair and wrinkles, a bent back and hollow cheeks will come to be regarded as mediaevally old-fashioned. The crone of the future will be golden, curly and cherry-lipped, neat-ankled and slender. The Portrait of the Artist's Mother will come to be almost indistinguishable, at future picture shows, from the Portrait of the Artist's Daughter. This desirable consummation will be due in part to skin foods and injections of paraffin-wax, facial surgery, mud baths, and paint, in part to improved health, due in its turn to a more rational mode of life. Ugliness is one of the symptoms of disease, beauty of health. In so far as the campaign for more beauty is also a campaign for more health, it is admirable and, up to a point, genuinely successful. Beauty that is merely the artificial shadow of these symptoms of health is intrinsically of poorer quality than the genuine article. Still, it is a sufficiently good imitation to be sometimes mistakable for the real thing. The apparatus for mimicking the symptoms of health is now within the reach of every moderately prosperous person; the knowledge of the way in which real health can be achieved is growing, and will in time, no doubt, be universally acted upon. When that happy moment comes, will every woman be beautiful—as beautiful, at any rate, as the natural shape of her features, with or without surgical and chemical aid, permits?

The answer is emphatically: No. For real beauty is as much an affair of the inner as of the outer self. The beauty of a porcelain jar is a matter of shape, of colour, of surface texture. The jar may be empty or tenanted by spiders, full of honey or stinking slime—it makes no difference to its beauty or ugliness. But a woman is alive, and her beauty is therefore not skin deep. The surface of the human vessel is affected by the nature of its spiritual contents. I have seen women who, by the standards of a connoisseur of porcelain, were ravishingly lovely. Their shape, their colour, their surface texture were perfect. And yet they were not beautiful. For the lovely vase was either empty or filled with some corruption. Spiritual emptiness or ugliness shows through. And conversely, there is an interior light that can transfigure forms that the pure aesthetician would regard as imperfect or downright ugly.

There are numerous forms of psychological ugliness. There is an ugliness of stupidity, for example, of unawareness (distressingly common among pretty women). An ugliness also of greed, of lasciviousness, of avarice. All the deadly sins, indeed, have their own peculiar negation of beauty. On the pretty faces of those especially who are trying to have a continuous 'good time,' one sees very often a kind of bored sullenness that ruins all their charm. I remember in particular two young American girls I once met in North Africa. From the porcelain specialist's point of view, they were beautiful. But the sullen boredom of which I have spoken was so deeply stamped into their fresh faces, their gait and gestures expressed so weary a listlessness, that it was unbearable to look at them. These exquisite creatures were positively repulsive.

Still commoner and no less repellent is the hardness which spoils so many pretty faces. Often, it is true, this air of hardness is due not to psychological causes, but to the contemporary habit of overpainting. In Paris, where this overpainting is most pronounced, many women have ceased to look human at all. Whitewashed and ruddled, they seem to be wearing masks. One must look closely to discover the soft and living face beneath. But often the face is not soft, often it turns out to be imperfectly alive. The hardness and deadness are from within. They are the outward and visible signs of some emotional or instinctive disharmony, accepted as a chronic condition of being. We do not need a Freudian to tell us that this disharmony is often of a sexual nature.

So long as such disharmonies continue to exist, so long as there is good reason for sullen boredom, so long as human beings allow themselves to be possessed and hag-ridden by monomaniacal vices, the cult of beauty is destined to be ineffectual. Successful in prolonging the appearance of youth, of realizing or simulating the symptoms of health, the campaign inspired by this cult remains fundamentally a failure. Its operations do not touch the deepest source of beauty—the experiencing soul. It is not by improving skin foods and point rollers, by cheapening health motors and electrical hair removers, that the human race will be made beautiful; it is not even by improving health. All men and women will be beautiful only when the social arrangements give to every one of them an opportunity to live completely and harmoniously, when there is no environmental incentive and no hereditary tendency towards monomaniacal vice. In other words, all men and women will never be beautiful. But there might easily be fewer ugly human beings in the world than there are at present. We must be content with moderate hopes.

THOSE PERSONAL TOUCHES

SOME little while ago old England was visited by an emissary from one of the most fabulously prosperous of American journals. I shall not divulge the journal's name. Suffice it to say that its circulation is an affair of millions and that the pages of advertising matter in every issue are, or were, before the slump, to be numbered by the hundred. The patient reader may discover, interspersed with the advertisements, a little healthy and uplifting fiction, a few articles.

It was in search of these last-mentioned commodities —articles—that the emissary came to England. In the course of an extended tour he must have visited almost all the literary men and women on the island. I had the honour of being among those visited. The journal is one, I am afraid, which seldom comes my way and which, even when it does come, I never read. (Life, after all, is so short, time flows so stanchlessly and there are so many interesting things to be done and seen and learnt, that one may be excused, I think, from perusing journals with circulations of over a million.) I do not know, therefore, what success attended the emissary's efforts to procure articles from England. All that I can say with certainty is that he has not yet received one from me. I wish he had; for then I should have received from him a very handsome cheque in return. I should have liked the money. The trouble was that I simply could not write the required article.

Now I have, in the course of a strenuous journalistic career, written articles on an extraordinary variety of subjects, from music to house decorating, from politics to painting, from plays to horticulture and metaphysics. Diffident at first of my powers, I learnt in the end to have confidence. I came to believe that I could, if called upon, write an article about anything. But I was wrong. The article which the emissary from the great American journal demanded of me was one, I found, which it was impossible for me to write. It was not that I was ignorant of the subject about which he asked me to hold forth. Ignorance is no deterrent to the hardened journalist, who knows by experience that an hour's reading in a well-stocked library will be enough to make him more learned about the matter in hand than ninety-nine out of every hundred of his readers. If it had been only a matter of ignorance, I should by this time have written a dozen articles and earned, I hope, a dozen cheques. No, it was not lack of knowledge that deterred me from writing. I was not ignorant of the subject of the proposed article. On the contrary, I knew a great deal about it—I knew perhaps too much. The emissary from the great American journal had asked me to write about myself.

Now there are certain aspects of myself about which I should feel no hesitation in writing. I should have no objection, for example, to explaining in print why I am not a Seventh Day Adventist, why I dislike playing bridge, why I prefer Chaucer as a poet to Keats. But the emissary of the great American journal did not want me to write about any of these aspects of myself. He wanted me to tell his million readers one of two things, either 'Why Women Are No Mystery To Me,' or 'Why Marriage Converted Me From My Belief In Free Love.' (I quote the actual formulae.) My protests that I had never believed in Free Love, that women were profoundly mysterious to me—no less mysterious, at any rate, than men, dogs, trees, stones, and all the other objects, living or inanimate, in this extraordinary world—were ignored. It was in vain that I proposed alternative titles; they were turned down at once and with decision. The million readers, it appeared, were interested in me only in so far as I had been initiated into the mysteries of Aphrodite, or converted from the worship of illicit Eros to that of Hymen. I thought of the handsome cheque and told the emissary from the great American journal that I would see what I could do to satisfy the million readers. That was long ago, and I have done nothing; I am afraid that I never shall. That handsome cheque will never find its way into my banking account.

What astonished and still astonishes me (though the wise man is astonished by nothing) is that similar handsome cheques should have found their way into the banking accounts of other literary men and women. For the earning of them seems to me personally an impossibility. The emissary from the great American journal himself admitted the difficulty of it. 'In writing personal confessions,' he epigrammatically put it, 'it's hard to strike the happy mean between reticence and bad taste.' And he cited, as an example of reticence, the case of a lady who had been married successively to a prize-fighter, a poet, an Italian duke, and a murderer, and whose personal confessions were yet entirely devoid of any 'human' interest whatever. I said nothing, but I reflected that my personal confessions, if I were to make them, would be no less completely lacking in the human, the all too human, touches demanded by the million readers. I have no objection to indulging in bad taste when I am writing about other people, particularly imaginary people. But with regard to myself, I can tolerate only reticence.

But not every one, it seems, shares my love of reticence. From the emissary of the great American journal, I gathered that no difficulty was experienced in finding literary men and women who were prepared to tell the world why their marriages were failures or successes, whichever the case might be; why they did, or didn't, practise birth control; why and on what experimental grounds they believed in polygamy or polyandry; and so on. As I have never read this particular great American journal, I cannot say what may have been disclosed, megaphonically, in its confessional. But from its emissary I gathered that there was almost nothing which had not been disclosed. These confessions, he further assured me, were very popular. The circulation had gone up by six hundred thousand since the publication of them had started. Readers, it seemed, found them very helpful. He gave me to understand that by writing at length and in detail why women were no mystery to me I should be doing a great Social Service, I should be a Benefactor of Humanity. The account of my experiences, he said, would help the million readers to solve their own soul-problems; my example would lighten them over dark and difficult stretches of Life's Road. And so on. Again I said nothing.

The hardest thing in the world is to understand, and, understanding, to allow for and forgive other people's tastes and other people's vices. Some people, for example, adore whisky, but would like to see all infringers of the seventh commandment thrown into prison and all who tell the truth about such infringements in print put to death. There are others, on the contrary, who love their neighbours' wives and the naked truth, and regard excessive drinkers with physical disgust and moral horror. Readers of magazine fiction find it hard to sympathize with those whose favourite reading is *The Critique of Pure Reason*. Nor can those whose hobby is astral physics easily understand the passion of so many of their fellow beings for watching football and betting on horse races. Similarly, since my own tastes run to reticence, I find it difficult to understand the confessor. To me he seems an exhibitionist, a monster of spiritual impudicity. For his part, I suppose, he finds me odiously selfish, unsociable, and misanthropic.

But the discussion of personal tastes is unfruitful. 'I like this,' asserts one; 'I like that,' says another. Each is obviously right, each is giving utterance to a truth that cannot be questioned, a truth that is beyond logic, immediate and compelling. Some authors like making public confessions; some don't. Those are the cardinal, personal truths of the matter. Fashion may a little modify personal inclination. More authors now resort to the confessional than resorted in the past. For Confession is fashionable, and the fashion is strong enough to make the writers whose tastes in this matter are neutral, swing over to the side of the unreticent.

The present modishness of self-revelation is only the latest symptom of that great tendency, manifest in recent history, for art to become more personal. In ancient times the arts were almost completely anonymous. The artist worked, but without expecting his labours to bring him personal fame or what is known as 'immortality.' Consider the retiring modesty of the Egyptian fresco painter who spent his life producing unsigned masterpieces in tombs, where no living eye was ever intended to see them. Primitive literature in all countries is shrouded in a similar anonymity.

It was the Greeks who first attached to works of art the names of their authors, and among whom it became customary for artists to work for the sake of immediate glory and immortal memory. It was among the Greeks that an interest in the personality of artists began to be widely felt. Several anecdotes illustrative of the characters and personal habits of Greek authors, painters, and sculptors have been preserved. The fall of the Roman Empire ushered in a second period of artistic anonymity. The Middle Ages produced a vast quantity of nameless painting, architecture, and sculpture, of ballads and narratives whose authors are unknown. And even of those artists whose names have come down to us very little has been recorded. Their contemporaries were not sufficiently interested in their private lives or personalities to set down the sort of details that it would have interested us to know.

With the Renaissance art once more ceased to be anonymous. Artists worked for contemporary celebrity and posthumous fame, and the public began to be interested in them as human beings, apart from their art. The autobiography of Benvenuto Cellini is a work symptomatic of the age in which it was written.

Since the days of the Renaissance public interest in the personality of artists has increased rather than diminished. And the artist, for his part, has done his best to satisfy this curiosity. In recent times it is from America that the demand for personal contacts with popular artists has been strongest, that curiosity about their intimate life has been most eager. The American public, it would seem, is not content to admire works of art; it wants to see and hear the artist in person. That is the principal reason, I suppose, why lectures are so enormously popular in America. The artists find this curiosity extremely profitable to themselves. From the time of Dickens onwards, authors have found that they could make more money by showing themselves and talking to American audiences than by going on writing books.

Increased demand for information about the private lives and characters of artists has led to an increased supply of autobiographies, reminiscences, and memoirs. Hundreds of people have made small fortunes by writing down what they remember of distinguished artists, and the artists have found it very profitable to play Boswell to their own Johnson. In the past, however, it has always been customary, except in rare cases, such as that of Rousseau, to pass over certain aspects of the intimate life in silence. A decent obscurity has generally veiled at least the nuptial chamber. It was an obscurity, I must admit, whose decency we have all had reasons to deplore. There are facts about the private lives of the departed Great which we would give much to know—facts which, owing to the silence of the Great themselves or of their friends, we shall never know. But this decent obscurity, it seems, is a thing already of the past. When great American journals start organizing the public demand for personal touches and inside information, there is not much hope for decency or obscurity. Persuaded by the dumb eloquence of handsome cheques, literary men and women have begun to tell the world their most intimate and amorous secrets. We know why X divorced his wife, how Y enjoyed her experiments in Harlem, what made young Z decide to become a monk, and so on. One wishes that a few great American journals had existed in Shakespeare's day. He might have contributed some interesting articles about Anne Hathaway and the Dark Lady of the Sonnets. He might; on the other hand he might not. And, much as I should like to know about Anne Hathaway and the Dark Lady, I rather hope he would not have written those articles. The only resemblance I have so far been able to discover between Shakespeare and myself is the fact that, like the Bard, I know little Latin and less Greek. I like to think that we also share a dislike for confession and a taste for reticence.

WANTED, A NEW PLEASURE

NINETEENTH-CENTURY science discovered the technique of discovery, and our age is, in consequence, the age of inventions. Yes, the age of inventions; we are never tired of proclaiming the fact. The age of inventions—and yet nobody has succeeded in inventing a new pleasure.

It was in the course of a recent visit to that region which the Travel Agency advertisements describe as the particular home of pleasure—the French Riviera—that this curious and rather distressing fact first dawned on me. From the Italian frontier to the mountains of the Esterel, forty miles of Mediterranean coast have been turned into one vast 'pleasure resort.' Or to be more accurate, they have been turned into one vast straggling suburb—the suburb of all Europe and the two Americas —punctuated here and there with urban nuclei, such as Mentone, Nice, Antibes, Cannes. The French have a genius for elegance; but they are also endowed with a genius for ugliness. There are no suburbs in the world so hideous as those which surround French cities. The great Mediterranean *banlieue* of the Riviera is no exception to the rule. The chaotic squalor of this long bourgeois slum is happily unique. The towns are greatly superior, of course, to their connecting suburbs. A certain pleasingly and absurdly old-fashioned, gimcrack grandiosity adorns Monte Carlo; Nice is large, bright, and lively; Cannes, gravely pompous and as though conscious of its expensive smartness. And all of them are equipped with the most elaborate and costly apparatus for providing their guests with pleasure.

It was while disporting myself, or rather while trying to disport myself, in the midst of this apparatus, that I came to my depressing conclusion about the absence of new pleasures. The thought, I remember, occurred to me one dismal winter evening as I emerged from the Restaurant des Ambassadeurs at Cannes into one of those howling winds, half Alpine, half marine, which on certain days transform the Croisette and the Promenade des Anglais into the most painfully realistic imitations of Wuthering Heights. I suddenly realized that, so far as pleasures were concerned, we are no better off than the Romans or the Egyptians. Galileo and Newton,

Faraday and Clerk Maxwell have lived, so far as human pleasures are concerned, in vain. The great joint-stock companies which control the modern pleasure industries can offer us nothing in any essential way different from the diversions which consuls offered to the Roman plebs or Trimalchio's panders could prepare for the amusement of the bored and jaded rich in the age of Nero. And this is true in spite of the movies, the talkies, the gramophone, the radio, and all similar modern apparatus for the entertainment of humanity. These instruments, it is true, are all essentially modern; nothing like them has existed before. But because the machines are modern it does not follow that the entertainments which they reproduce and broadcast are also modern. They are not. All that these new machines do is to make accessible to a larger public the drama, pantomime, and music which have from time immemorial amused the leisured of humanity.

These mechanically reproduced entertainments are cheap and are therefore not encouraged in pleasure resorts, such as those on the Riviera, which exist for the sole purpose of making travellers part with the maximum amount of money in the minimum space of time. In these places drama, pantomime, and music are therefore provided in the original form, as they were provided to our ancestors, without the interposition of any mechanical go-between. The other pleasures of the resorts are no less traditional. Eating and drinking too much; looking at half or wholly naked ballerinas and acrobats in the hope of stimulating a jaded sexual appetite; dancing; playing games and watching games, preferably rather bloody and ferocious games; killing animals—these have always been the sports of the rich and, when they had the chance, of the poor also. No less traditional is that other strange amusement so characteristic of the Riviera—gambling. Gambling must be at least as old as money; much older, I should imagine—as old as human nature itself, or at any rate as old as boredom, as old as the craving for artificial excitement and factitious emotions.

Officially, this closes the list of pleasures provided by the Riviera entertainment industries. But it must not be forgotten that, for those who pay for them, all these pleasures are situated, so to speak, in a certain emotional field—in the pleasure-pain complex of snobbery. The fact of being able to buy admission to 'exclusive' (that is generally to say, expensive) places of entertainment gives most people a considerable satisfaction. They like to think of the poor and vulgar herd outside, just as, according to Tertullian and many other Fathers of the Church, the Blessed enjoy looking down from the balconies of Heaven on to the writhings of the Damned in the pit below. They like to feel, with a certain swelling of pride, that they are sitting among the elect, or that they are themselves the elect, whose names figure in the social columns of the Continental *Daily Mail,* or the Paris edition of the New York *Herald.* True, snobbery is often the source of excruciating pain. But it is no less the source of exquisite pleasures. These pleasures, I repeat, are liberally provided in all the resorts and constitute a kind of background to all the other pleasures.

Now all these pleasure-resort pleasures, including those of snobbery, are immemorially antique—variations, at the best, on traditional themes. We live in the age of inventions; but the professional discoverers have been unable to think of any wholly new way of pleasurably stimulating our senses or evoking agreeable emotional reactions.

But this, I went on to reflect, as I shouldered my way through the opposing gale on the Croisette, this is not, after all, so surprising. Our physiological make-up has remained very much what it was ten thousand years ago. True, there have been considerable changes in our mode of consciousness; at no time, it is obvious, are *all* the potentialities of the human psyche simultaneously realized; history is, among many other things, the record of the successive actualization, neglect, and reactualization in another context of different sets of these almost indefinitely numerous potentialities. But in spite of these changes (which it is customary to call, incorrectly, psychic evolution), the simple instinctive feelings to which, as well as to the senses, the purveyors of pleasure make their appeal, have remained remarkably stable. The task of the pleasure merchants is to provide a sort of Highest Common Denominator of entertainment that shall satisfy large numbers of men and women, irrespective of their psychological idiosyncrasies. Such an entertainment, it is obvious, must be very unspecialized. Its appeal must be to the simplest of shared human characteristics—to the physiological and psychological foundations of personality, not to personality itself. Now, the number of appeals that can be made to what I may call the Great Impersonalities common to all human beings is strictly limited—so strictly limited that, as it has turned out, our inventors have been unable hitherto to devise any new ones. (One doubtful example of a new pleasure exists; I shall speak of it later.) We are still content with the pleasures which charmed our ancestors in the Bronze Age. (Incidentally, there are good reasons for regarding our entertainments as intrinsically inferior to those of the Bronze Age. Modern pleasures are wholly secular and without the smallest cosmic significance; whereas the entertainments of the Bronze Age were mostly religious rites and were felt by those who participated in them to be pregnant with important meanings.)

So far as I can see, the only possible new pleasure would be one derived from the invention of a new drug —of a more efficient and less harmful substitute for alcohol and cocaine. If I were a millionaire, I should endow a band of research workers to look for the ideal intoxicant. If we could sniff or swallow something that would, for five or six hours each day, abolish our solitude as individuals, atone us with our fellows in a glowing exaltation of affection and make life in all its aspects seem not only worth living, but divinely beautiful and significant, and if this heavenly, world-transfiguring drug were of such a kind that we could wake up next morning with a clear head and an undamaged constitution—then, it seems to me, all our problems (and not merely the one small problem of discovering a novel pleasure) would be wholly solved and earth would become paradise.

The nearest approach to such a new drug—and how immeasurably remote it is from the ideal intoxicant!— is the drug of speed. Speed, it seems to me, provides the one genuinely modern pleasure. True, men have always enjoyed speed; but their enjoyment has been limited, until very recent times, by the capacities of the horse, whose maximum velocity is not much more than thirty miles an hour. Now thirty miles an hour on a horse *feels* very much faster than sixty miles an hour in a train or a hundred in an aëroplane. The train is too large and steady, the aëroplane too remote from stationary surroundings, to give their passengers a very intense sensation of speed. The automobile is sufficiently small and sufficiently near the ground to be able to compete, as an intoxicating speed-purveyor, with the galloping horse. The inebriating effects of speed are noticeable, on horseback, at about twenty miles an hour, in a car at about sixty. When the car has passed seventy-two, or thereabouts, one begins to feel an unprecedented sensation—a sensation which no man in the days of horses ever felt. It grows intenser with every increase of velocity. I myself have never travelled at much more than eighty miles an hour in a car; but those who have drunk a stronger brewage of this strange intoxicant tell me that new marvels await any one who has the opportunity of passing the hundred mark. At what point the pleasure turns into pain, I do not know. Long before the fantastic Daytona figures are reached, at any rate. Two hundred miles an hour must be absolute torture.

But in this, of course, speed is like all other pleasures; indulged in to excess, they become their opposites. Each particular pleasure has its corresponding particular pain, boredom, or disgust. The compensating drawback of too much speed-pleasure must be, I suppose, a horrible compound of intense physical discomfort and intense fear. No; if one must go in for excesses one would probably be better advised to be old-fashioned and stick to overeating.

SERMONS IN CATS

I MET, not long ago, a young man who aspired to become a novelist. Knowing that I was in the profession, he asked me to tell him how he should set to work to realize his ambition. I did my best to explain. 'The first thing,' I said, 'is to buy quite a lot of paper, a bottle of ink, and a pen. After that you merely have to write.' But this was not enough for my young friend. He seemed to have a notion that there was some sort of esoteric cookery book, full of literary recipes, which you had only to follow attentively to become a Dickens, a Henry James, a Flaubert—'according to taste,' as the authors of recipes say, when they come to the question of seasoning and sweetening. Wouldn't I let him have a glimpse of this cookery book? I said that I was sorry, but that (unhappily—for what an endless amount of time and trouble it would save!) I had never even seen such a work. He seemed sadly disappointed; so, to console the poor lad, I advised him to apply to the professors of dramaturgy and short-story writing at some reputable university; if any one possessed a trustworthy cookery book of literature, it should surely be they. But even this was not enough to satisfy the young man. Disappointed in his hope that I would give him the fictional equivalent of 'One Hundred Ways of Cooking Eggs' or the 'Carnet de la Ménagère,' he began to cross-examine me about my methods of 'collecting material.' Did I keep a notebook or a daily journal? Did I jot down thoughts and phrases in a card-index? Did I systematically frequent the drawing-rooms of the rich and fashionable? Or did I, on the contrary, inhabit the Sussex downs? or spend my evenings looking for 'copy' in East End gin-palaces? Did I think it was wise to frequent the company of intellectuals? Was it a good thing for a writer of novels to try to be well educated, or should he confine his reading exclusively to other novels? And so on. I did my best to reply to these questions—as non-committally, of course, as I could. And as the young man still looked rather disappointed, I volunteered a final piece of advice, gratuitously. 'My young friend,' I said, 'if you want to be a psychological novelist and write about human beings, the best thing you can do is to keep a pair of cats.' And with that I left him.

I hope, for his own sake, that he took my advice. For

it was good advice—the fruit of much experience and many meditations. But I am afraid that, being a rather foolish young man, he merely laughed at what he must have supposed was only a silly joke: laughed, as I myself foolishly laughed when, years ago, that charming and talented and extraordinary man, Ronald Firbank, once told me that he wanted to write a novel about life in Mayfair and so was just off to the West Indies to look for copy among the negroes. I laughed at the time; but I see now that he was quite right Primitive people, like children and animals, are simply civilized people with the lid off, so to speak—the heavy elaborate lid of manners, conventions, traditions of thought and feeling beneath which each one of us passes his or her existence. This lid can be very conveniently studied in Mayfair, shall we say, or Passy, or Park Avenue. But what goes on underneath the lid in these polished and elegant districts? Direct observation (unless we happen to be endowed with a very penetrating intuition) tells us but little; and, if we cannot infer what is going on under other lids from what we see, introspectively, by peeping under our own, then the best thing we can do is to take the next boat for the West Indies, or else, less expensively, pass a few mornings in the nursery, or alternatively, as I suggested to my literary young friend, buy a pair of cats.

Yes, a pair of cats. Siamese by preference; for they are certainly the most 'human' of all the race of cats. Also the strangest, and, if not the most beautiful, certainly the most striking and fantastic. For what disquieting pale blue eyes stare out from the black velvet mask of their faces! Snow-white at birth, their bodies gradually darken to a rich mulatto colour. Their forepaws are gloved almost to the shoulder like the long black kid arms of Yvette Guilbert; over their hind legs are tightly drawn the black silk stockings with which Félicien Rops so perversely and indecently clothed his pearly nudes. Their tails, when they have tails—and I would always recommend the budding novelist to buy the tailed variety; for the tail, in cats, is the principal organ of emotional expression and a Manx cat is the equivalent of a dumb man—their tails are tapering black serpents endowed, even when the body lies in Sphinx-like repose, with a spasmodic and uneasy life of their own. And what strange voices they have! Sometimes like the complaining of small children; sometimes like the noise of lambs; sometimes like the agonized and furious howling of lost souls. Compared with these fantastic creatures, other cats, however beautiful and engaging, are apt to seem a little insipid.

Well, having bought his cats, nothing remains for the would-be novelist but to watch them living from day to day; to mark, learn, and inwardly digest the lessons about human nature which they teach; and finally—for, alas, this arduous and unpleasant necessity always arises—finally write his book about Mayfair, Passy, or Park Avenue, whichever the case may be.

Let us consider some of these instructive sermons in cats, from which the student of human psychology can learn so much. We will begin—as every good novel should begin, instead of absurdly ending—with marriage. The marriage of Siamese cats, at any rate as I have observed it, is an extraordinarily dramatic event. To begin with, the introduction of the bridegroom to his bride (I am assuming that, as usually happens in the world of cats, they have not met before their wedding day) is the signal for a battle of unparalleled ferocity. The young wife's first reaction to the advances of her would-be husband is to fly at his throat. One is thankful, as one watches the fur flying and listens to the piercing yells of rage and hatred, that a kindly providence has not allowed these devils to grow any larger. Waged between creatures as big as men, such battles would bring death and destruction to everything within a radius of hundreds of yards. As things are, one is able, at the risk of a few scratches, to grab the combatants by the scruffs of their necks and drag them, still writhing and spitting, apart. What would happen if the newly-wedded pair were allowed to go on fighting to the bitter end I do not know, and have never had the scientific curiosity or the strength of mind to try to find out. I suspect that, contrary to what happened in Hamlet's family, the wedding baked meats would soon be serving for a funeral. I have always prevented this tragical consummation by simply shutting up the bride in a room by herself and leaving the bridegroom for a few hours to languish outside the door. He does not languish dumbly; but for a long time there is no answer, save an occasional hiss or growl, to his melancholy cries of love. When, finally, the bride begins replying in tones as soft and yearning as his own, the door may be opened. The bridegroom darts in and is received, not with tooth and claw as on the former occasion, but with every demonstration of affection.

At first sight there would seem, in this specimen of feline behaviour, no special 'message' for humanity. But appearances are deceptive; the lids under which civilized people live are so thick and so profusely sculptured with mythological ornaments, that it is difficult to recognize the fact, so much insisted upon by D. H. Lawrence in his novels and stories, that there is almost always a mingling of hate with the passion of love and that young girls very often feel (in spite of their sentiments and even their desires) a real abhorrence of the fact of physical love. Unlidded, the cats make manifest this ordinarily obscure mystery of human nature. After witnessing a cats' wedding no young novelist can rest content with the falsehood and banalities which pass, in current fiction, for descriptions of love.

Time passes and, their honeymoon over, the cats begin to tell us things about humanity which even the lid of civilization cannot conceal in the world of men. They tell us—what, alas, we already know—that husbands soon tire of their wives, particularly when they are expecting or nursing families; that the essence of maleness is the love of adventure and infidelity; that guilty consciences and good resolutions are the psychological symptoms of that disease which spasmodically affects practically every male between the ages of eighteen and sixty—the disease called 'the morning after'; and that with the disappearance of the disease the psychological symptoms also disappear, so that when temptation comes again, conscience is dumb and good resolutions count for nothing. All these unhappily too familiar truths are illustrated by the cats with a most comical absence of disguise. No man has ever dared to manifest his boredom so insolently as does a Siamese tom-cat, when he yawns in the face of his amorously importunate wife. No man has ever dared to proclaim his illicit amours so frankly as this same tom caterwauling on the tiles. And how slinkingly—no man was ever so abject—he returns next day to the conjugal basket by the fire! You can measure the guiltiness of his conscience by the angle of his back-pressed ears, the droop of his tail. And when, having sniffed him and so discovered his infidelity, his wife, as she always does on these occasions, begins to scratch his face (already scarred, like a German student's, with the traces of a hundred duels), he makes no attempt to resist; for, self-convicted of sin, he knows that he deserves all he is getting.

It is impossible for me in the space at my disposal to enumerate all the human truths which a pair of cats can reveal or confirm. I will cite only one more of the innumerable sermons in cats which my memory holds—an acted sermon which, by its ludicrous pantomime, vividly brought home to me the most saddening peculiarity of our human nature, its irreducible solitariness. The circumstances were these. My she-cat, by now a wife of long standing and several times a mother, was passing through one of her occasional phases of amorousness. Her husband, now in the prime of life and parading that sleepy arrogance which is the characteristic of the mature and conquering male (he was now the feline equivalent of some herculean young Alcibiades of the Guards), refused to have anything to do with her.

It was in vain that she uttered her love-sick mewing, in vain that she walked up and down in front of him rubbing herself voluptuously against doors and chair-legs as she passed, it was in vain that she came and licked his face. He shut his eyes, he yawned, he averted his head, or, if she became too importunate, got up and slowly, with an insulting air of dignity and detachment, stalked away. When the opportunity presented itself, he escaped and spent the next twenty-four hours upon the tiles. Left to herself, the wife went wandering disconsolately about the house, as though in search of a vanished happiness, faintly and plaintively mewing to herself in a voice and with a manner that reminded one irresistibly of Mélisande in Debussy's opera. '*Je ne suis pas heureuse ici*,' she seemed to be saying. And, poor little beast, she wasn't. But, like her big sisters and brothers of the human world, she had to bear her unhappiness in solitude, uncomprehended, unconsoled. For in spite of language, in spite of intelligence and intuition and sympathy, one can never really communicate anything to anybody. The essential substance of every thought and feeling remains incommunicable, locked up in the impenetrable strong-room of the individual soul and body. Our life is a sentence of perpetual solitary confinement. This mournful truth was overwhelmingly borne in on me as I watched the abandoned and love-sick cat as she walked unhappily round my room. '*Je ne suis pas heureuse ici,*' she kept mewing, '*je ne suis pas heureuse ici.*' And her expressive black tail would lash the air in a tragical gesture of despair. But each time it twitched, hop-la! from under the armchair, from behind the book-case, wherever he happened to be hiding at the moment, out jumped her only son (the only one, that is, we had not given away), jumped like a ludicrous toy tiger, all claws out, on to the moving tail. Sometimes he would miss, sometimes he caught it, and getting the tip between his teeth would pretend to worry it, absurdly ferocious. His mother would have to jerk it violently to get it out of his mouth. Then, he would go back under his armchair again and, crouching down, his hindquarters trembling, would prepare once more to spring. The tail, the tragical, despairingly gesticulating tail, was for him the most irresistible of playthings. The patience of the mother was angelical. There was never a rebuke or a punitive reprisal; when the child became too intolerable, she just moved away; that was all. And meanwhile, all the time, she went on mewing, plaintively, despairingly. '*Je ne suis pas heureuse ici, je ne suis pas heureuse ici.*' It was heartbreaking. The more so as the antics of the kitten were so extraordinarily ludicrous. It was as though a slap-stick comedian had broken in on the lamentations of Mélisande—not mischievously, not wittingly, for there was not the smallest intention to hurt in the little cat's performance, but simply from lack of comprehension. Each was alone serving his life-sentence of solitary confinement. There was no communication from cell to cell. Absolutely no communication. These sermons in cats can be exceedingly depressing.

SECTION V

VULGARITY IN LITERATURE
DIGRESSIONS FROM A THEME

THE difficulty, when one is using words of appraisal, the difficulty of knowing what one means!

Then why, if it is so hard, make any attempt to know? Would it not be wiser to follow the example of that Geneva Conference convened, not long ago, to consider means for the suppression of the traffic in obscene publications? For when the Greek delegate (too Socratic by half) suggested that it might be a good thing to establish a preliminary definition of the word 'obscene,' Sir Archibald Bodkin sprang to his feet with a protest. 'There is no definition of indecent or obscene in English Statute Law.' The law of other countries being, apparently, no more explicit, it was unanimously decided that no definition was possible. After which, having triumphantly asserted that they did not know what they were talking about, the members of the Congress settled down to their discussion.

My business is not with the obscene, but with the vulgar. When I call something or somebody 'vulgar,' what *precisely* (as Mr. T. S. Eliot would critically ask) am I saying? Rushing in where Sir Archibald and his colleagues so wisely feared to tread, I shall try to discover.

To begin with, then, I find that there are many occasions when, strictly speaking, I *mean* nothing at all, but am using the word merely to express a dislike—as a term of abuse, a politer synonym, shall we say, of 'bloody.' On such occasions 'vulgar' is no more than a vaguely pejorative noise. More often, however, I find that I intend to *say* something when I employ the word, not merely to snarl.

In certain circumstances, for example, I use the word in its strict etymological sense. When I say that a man has a vulgar accent or vulgar table manners, I mean that his accent and his manners remind me of those current in the lower ranks of society—of the particular society in which I happen to live. For vulgar here is not necessarily vulgar there. *Eructavit cor meum.* East of Constantinople, the action is said to be polite. Here, Sir Toby Belch, though a knight, can never have moved in the highest circles. Or, yes; on second thoughts, he conceivably might have. For the standards of vulgarity are seen to change as you move vertically upwards through the strata of a single society, just as they change before

VULGARITY IN LITERATURE 245

the eyes of a spectator moving horizontally from one society to another. What is vulgar on high level A may have ceased to be vulgar on the yet higher level B. There are refinements beyond refinements, almost *ad infinitum*. Like Paradise, the *Monde* itself has its high and low. Proust is the Dante of these high mundane spheres; but while it took several centuries to reduce Dante's guide-book to out-of-dateness, Proust's is already, in its factual details (though not, of course, in its spirit), as hopelessly behind the times as a pre-war Baedeker. The social heavens are for ever changing.

But these relativities are too obvious to be very interesting. The Absolute chimerically beckons; and, though we can never hope to come up with it, the chase may be amusing in itself and, who knows? by the way we may actually catch a hare or two, smaller indeed and less noble than the quarry we are after, but having at least the merit of solidly existing, of being visibly there.

We have considered, so far, two cases: the case in which the word 'vulgar' says, 'I don't like this,' and the case in which it says, 'This reminds me of what are, to me, the lower classes.' In the case we are about to consider now, 'vulgar' says something less easily definable. For instance, I can assert that 'This man is vulgar. The fact that he is of good family and was educated at the right places makes no difference. He is vulgar, intrinsically.' What *precisely* do I mean here?

Etymology is helpful even in this case. The vulgar man of good family is not, indeed, a member of the lower classes in our actual society. But there is an ideal society, in which, we feel, he and his like belong to some very squalid caste.

No values, except perhaps the most rudimentary biological values, are accepted by all human beings. Only the tendency to evaluate is universal. In other words, the machinery for creating values is given, but the values themselves must be manufactured. The process has not yet been rationalized; value-making is still a village industry. Among the educated classes in the West, however, values are sufficiently nearly standardized for us to be able to speak about the ideal society as though it were an absolute.

The extremes of vulgarity are as rare as the extremes of goodness, wickedness, or genius; but it happens occasionally that we meet a nature's non-gentleman who is obviously one of the pariahs of our ideal society. Such people are, intrinsically, what those wretched Indians who sweep the floor and empty the slops are by accident —untouchable. In India, when you leave your hotel and want to tip the sweeper, you must not hold out the coin, expecting him to take it. His immediate reaction to your gesture will be to shrink away; for if your fingers were to touch his receiving palm you would be defiled. He is considerately sparing you the trouble of having to take a bath, fumigate yourself, and change your underclothing. The tipping of sweepers has its own special technique; you must halt several yards away from your expectant beneficiary and throw your gift on to the ground at his feet. Commercial transactions during the Black Death must have been carried on in much the same style.

Training has taught the accidentally untouchable Indian to realize his own defiling lowness and to act accordingly. Would that nature had done the same for the intrinsic outcastes of our ideal society! But, alas, she hasn't. You find yourself at dinner sitting next to X, the eminent politician; the journalist, Y, is at large and invites you to his favourite public house. Unlike the sweepers of India, these intrinsic outcastes do not play their untouchable's part. So far are they from knowing their places, that they actually think they are doing you an honour by sitting at your table, a kindness by offering you, before lunch and in some stinking bar parlour, a double whisky or a noggin of glutinous port. As for shrinking, they do not dream of it; on the contrary, they push themselves forward. Indeed, a certain loud self-satisfaction (which renders it impossible for one to feel much sympathy with the intrinsic untouchable in his affliction), a certain thrusting and pretentious vanity is, as I shall have many occasions of showing in the course of these digressions, one of the essential elements of vulgarity. Vulgarity is a lowness that proclaims itself—and the self-proclamation is also intrinsically a lowness. For pretentiousness in whatever field, unless more than justified by native capacity and demonstrable achievement, is low in itself. Moreover, it underlines all other deficiencies and, as a suitable chemical will reveal words written in invisible ink, calls out the latent lownesses in a character, so that they manifest themselves in the form of open vulgarities.

There is a vulgarity in the sphere of morals, a vulgarity of emotions and intellect, a vulgarity even of the spirit. A man can be wicked, or stupid, or passionate without being vulgar. He can also be vulgarly good, vulgarly intelligent, vulgarly emotional or unemotional, vulgarly spiritual. Moreover, he can belong to the highest class in one sphere of activity and yet be low in another. I have known men of the greatest intellectual refinement, whose emotional life was repugnantly vulgar. Each one of us is like the population of a town built on the slope of a hill: we exist simultaneously at many different levels.

These brief notes on personal vulgarity are meant to

serve as an introduction to what I propose to say about vulgarity in literature. Letters, life—the two worlds are parallel. What is true here is true, with a difference, there. For the sake of completeness I ought, of course, to have illustrated my generalizations about vulgarity in life with concrete examples. But this would have meant an excursion into the realm of fiction, or historical biography—or contemporary libel. I should have had to create a set of artistically living characters, with the circumstances of their existence. World and time, as usual, were lacking. Besides, as it happens, I have, in several works of fiction, elaborately exemplified emotional and intellectual vulgarity as revealed in life—perhaps also, without meaning to, as they are revealed in letters! I shall not begin again here. Here the ready-made examples of vulgarity provided by literature will serve, retrospectively and by analogy, to illustrate my generalizations about vulgarity in life.

§ II

VULGARITY in literature must be distinguished from the vulgarity inherent in the profession of letters. Every man is born with his share of Original Sin, to which every writer adds a pinch of Original Vulgarity. Necessarily and quite inevitably. For exhibitionism is always vulgar, even if what you exhibit is the most exquisitely refined of souls.

Some writers are more squeamishly conscious than others of the essential vulgarity of their trade—so much so, that, like Flaubert, they have found it hard to commit that initial offence against good breeding: the putting of pen to paper.

It is just possible, of course, that the greatest writers have never written; that the world is full of Monsieur Testes and mute inglorious Miltons, too delicate to come before the public. I should like to believe it; but I find it hard. Your great writer is possessed by a devil, over which he has very little control. If the devil wants to come out (and, in practice, devils always do want to come out), it will do so, however loud the protests of the aristocratic consciousness, with which it uneasily cohabits. The profession of literature may be 'fatally marred by a secret absurdity'; the devil simply doesn't care. *Scribo quia absurdum.*

§ III

To be pale, to have no appetite, to swoon at the slightest provocation—these, not so long ago, were the signs of maidenly good breeding. In other words, when a girl was marked with the stigmata of anaemia and chronic constipation, you knew she was a lady. Virtues are generally fashioned (more or less elegantly, according to the skill of the moral *couturier*) out of necessities. Rich girls had no need to work; the aristocratic tradition discouraged them from voluntarily working; and the Christian tradition discouraged them from compromising their maiden modesty by taking anything like violent exercise. Good carriage-roads and, finally, railways spared them the healthy fatigues of riding. The virtues of Fresh Air had not yet been discovered and the Draught was still the commonest, as it was almost the most dangerous, manifestation of the Diabolic Principle. More perverse than Chinese foot-squeezers, the topiarists of European fashion had decreed that the elegant should have all her viscera constricted and displaced by tight lacing. In a word, the rich girl lived a life scientifically calculated to make her unhealthy. A virtue was made of humiliating necessity, and the pale ethereal swooner of romantic literature remained for years the type and mirror of refined young womanhood.

Something of the same kind happens from time to time in the realm of literature. Moments come when too conspicuous a show of vigour, too frank an interest in common things are signs of literary vulgarity. To be really lady-like, the Muses, like their mortal sisters, must be anaemic and constipated. On the more sensitive writers of certain epochs circumstances impose an artistic wasting away, a literary consumption. This distressing fatality is at once transformed into a virtue, which it becomes a duty for all to cultivate.

'*Vivre? Nos valets le feront pour nous.*' For, oh, the vulgarity of it! The vulgarity of this having to walk and talk; to open and close the eyes; to think and drink and every day, yes, every day, to eat, eat and excrete. And then this having to pursue the female of one's species, or the male, whichever the case may be; this having to cerebrate, to calculate, to copulate, to propagate. . . . No, no—too gross, too stupidly low. Such things, as Villiers de l'Isle-Adam says, are all very well for footmen. But for a descendant of how many generations of Templars, of Knights of Rhodes and of Malta, Knights of the Garter and the Holy Ghost and all the variously coloured Eagles—obviously, it was out of the question; it simply wasn't done. *Vivre? Nos valets le feront pour nous.*

At the same point, but on another plane, of the great spiral of history, Prince Gotama, more than two thousand years before, had also discovered the vulgarity of living. The sight of a corpse rotting by the roadside had set him thinking. It was his first introduction to death. Now, a corpse, poor thing, is an untouchable and the process of decay is, of all pieces of bad manners, the vulgarest imaginable. For a corpse is, by definition, a person absolutely devoid of *savoir vivre*. Even your sweeper knows better. But in every greatest king, in every loveliest flowery princess, in every poet most refined, every best dressed dandy, every holiest and most spiritual teacher, there lurks, waiting, waiting for the moment to emerge, an outcaste of the outcastes, a dung carrier, a dog, lower than the lowest, bottomlessly vulgar.

What with making their way and enjoying what they have won, heroes have no time to think. But the sons of heroes—ah, they have all the necessary leisure. The future Buddha belonged to the generation which has time. He saw the corpse, he smelt it vulgarly stinking, he thought. The echoes of his meditations still reverberate, rich with an accumulated wealth of harmonics, like the memory of the organ's final chord pulsing back and forth under the vaulting of a cathedral.

No less than that of war or statecraft, the history of economics has its heroic ages. Economically, the nineteenth century was the equivalent of those brave times about which we read in Beowulf and the Iliad. Its heroes struggled, conquered or were conquered, and had no time to think. Its bards, the Romantics, sang rapturously, not of the heroes, but of higher things (for they were Homers who detested Achilles), sang with all the vehemence which one of the contemporary heroes would have put into grinding the faces of the poor. It was only in the second and third generation that men began to have leisure and the necessary detachment to find the whole business—economic heroism and romantic bardism—rather vulgar. Villiers, like Gotama, was one who had time. That he was the descendant of all those Templars and Knights of this and that was, to a great extent, irrelevant. The significant fact was this: he was, or at any rate chronologically might have been, the son and grandson of economic heroes and romantic bards—a man of the decadence. Sons have always a rebellious wish to be disillusioned by that which charmed their fathers; and, wish or no wish, it was difficult for a sensitive man to see and smell the already putrefying corpse of industrial civilization and not be shocked by it into distressful thought. Villiers was duly shocked; and he expressed his shockedness in terms of an aristocratic disdain that was almost Brahminical in its intensity. But his feudal terminology was hardly more than an accident. Born without any of Villiers' perhaps legendary advantages of breeding, other sensitives of the same post-heroic generation were just as profoundly shocked. The scion of Templars had a more striking vocabulary than the others—that was all. For the most self-conscious and intelligent artists of the last decades of the nineteenth century, too frank an acceptance of the obvious actualities of life, too hearty a manner and (to put it grossly) too many 'guts' were rather vulgar. *Vivre? Nos valets le feront pour nous.* (Incidentally, the suicide rate took a sharp upward turn during the 'sixties. In some countries it is nearly five times what it was seventy years ago.) Zola was the master footman of the age. That vulgar interest in actual life! And all those guts of his—was the man preparing to set up as a tripe-dresser?

A few ageing ninetyites survive; a few young neo-ninetyites, who judge of art and all other human activities in terms of the Amusing and the Tiresome, play kittenishly around with their wax flowers and stuffed owls and Early Victorian beadwork. But, old and young, they are insignificant. Guts and an acceptance of the actual are no longer vulgar. Why not? What has happened? Three things: the usual reaction of sons against fathers, another industrial revolution and a rediscovery of mystery. We have entered (indeed, we have perhaps already passed through) a second heroic age of economics. Its Homers, it is true, are almost without exception sceptical, ironic, denunciatory. But this scepticism, this irony, this denunciation are as lively and vehement as that which is doubted and denounced. Babbitt infects even his detractors with some of his bouncing vitality.

The Romantics, in the same way, possessed an energy proportionate to that of their enemies, the economic heroes who were creating modern industrialism. Life begets life, even in opposition to itself.

Vivre? Nos valets le feront pour nous. But the physicists and psychologists have revealed the universe as a place, in spite of everything, so fantastically queer, that to hand it over to be enjoyed by footmen would be a piece of gratuitous humanitarianism. Servants must not be spoiled. The most refined spirits need not be ashamed in taking a hearty interest in the rediscovered mystery of the actual world. True, it is a sinister as well as a fascinating and mysterious world. And what a mess, with all our good intentions, we have made and are busily making of our particular corner of it! The same old industrial corpse—to some extent disinfected and galvanically stimulated at the moment into a twitching semblance of healthy life—still rots by the wayside, as it rotted in Villiers' time. And as for Gotama's carrion—that of course is always with us. There are, as ever, excellent reasons for personal despair; while the reasons for despairing about society are actually a good deal more cogent than at most times. A Mallarméan shrinking away into pure poetry, a delicate Henry-Jamesian avoidance of all the painful issues would seem to be justified. But the spirit of the time—the industrially heroic time in which we live—is opposed to these retirements, these handings over of life to footmen. It demands that we should 'press with strenuous tongue against our palate' not only joy's grape, but every Dead Sea fruit. Even dust and ashes must be relished with gusto. Thus, modern American fiction, like the modern American fact which it so accurately renders, is ample and lively. And yet, 'Dust and ashes, dust and ashes' is the fundamental theme and final moral of practically every modern American novel of any distinction. High spirits and a heroic vitality are put into the expression of despair. The hopelessness is almost Rabelaisian.

§ IV

IT WAS vulgar at the beginning of the nineteenth century to mention the word 'handkerchief' on the French tragic stage. An arbitrary convention had decreed that tragic personages must inhabit a world, in which noses exist only to distinguish the noble Romans from the Greeks and Hebrews, never to be blown. Arbitrary conventions of one sort or another are essential to art. But as the sort of convention constantly varies, so does the corresponding vulgarity. We are back among the relativities.

In the case of the handkerchief we have a particular and rather absurd application of a very widely accepted artistic convention. This convention is justified by the ancient metaphysical doctrine, which distinguishes in the universe two principles, mind and matter, and which attributes to mind an immeasurable superiority. In the name of this principle many religions have demanded the sacrifice of the body; their devotees have responded by mortifying the flesh and, in extreme cases, by committing self-castration and even suicide. Literature has its Manichaeans as well as religion: men who on principle would exile the body and its functions from the world of their art, who condemn as vulgar all too particular and detailed accounts of physical actuality, as vulgar any attempt to relate mental or spiritual events to happenings in the body. The inhabitants of their universe are not human beings, but the tragical heroes and heroines who never blow their noses.

Artistically, the abolition of handkerchiefs and all that handkerchiefs directly or indirectly stand for has certain advantages. The handkerchiefless world of pure mind and spirit is, for an adult, the nearest approach to that infinitely comfortable Freudian womb, towards which, as towards a lost paradise, we are always nostalgically yearning. In the handkerchiefless mental world we are at liberty to work things out to their logical con-

VULGARITY IN LITERATURE 259

clusions, we can guarantee the triumph of justice, we can control the weather and (in the words of those yearning popular songs which are the national anthems of Wombland) make our Dreams come True by living under Skies of Blue with You. Nature in the mental world is not that collection of tiresomely opaque and recalcitrant objects, so bewildering to the man of science, so malignantly hostile to the man of action; it is the luminously rational substance of a Hegelian nature-philosophy, a symbolic manifestation of the principles of dialectic. Artistically, such a Nature is much more satisfactory (because so much more easy to deal with) than the queer, rather sinister and finally quite incomprehensible monster, by which, when we venture out of our ivory towers, we are instantly swallowed. And man, than whom, as Sophocles long since remarked, nothing is more monstrous, more marvellous, more terrifyingly strange (it is hard to find a single word to render his *deinoteron*)—man, too, is a very unsatisfactory subject for literature. For this creature of inconsistencies can live on too many planes of existence. He is the inhabitant of a kind of psychological Woolworth Building; you never know—he never knows himself—which floor he'll step out at to-morrow, nor even whether, a minute from now, he won't take it into his head to jump into the elevator and shoot up a dozen or down perhaps twenty stories into some totally different mode of being. The effect of the Manichaean condemnation of the body is at once to reduce this impossible skyscraper to less than half its original height. Confined henceforward to the mental floors of his being, man becomes an almost easily manageable subject for the writer. In the French tragedies (the most completely Manichaean works of art ever created) lust itself has ceased to be corporeal and takes its place among the other abstract symbols, with which the authors write their strange algebraical equations of passion and conflict. The beauty of algebraical symbols lies in their universality; they stand not for one particular case, but for all cases. Manichaeans, the classical writers confined themselves exclusively to the study of man as a creature of pure reason and discarnate passions. Now the body particularizes and separates, the mind unites. By the very act of imposing limitations the classicists were enabled to achieve a certain universality of statement impossible to those who attempt to reproduce the particularities and incompletenesses of actual corporeal life. But what they gained in universality, they lost in vivacity and immediate truth. You cannot get something for nothing. Some people think that universality can be paid for too highly.

To enforce their ascetic code the classicists had to

devise a system of critical sanctions. Chief among these was the stigma of vulgarity attached to all those who insisted too minutely on the physical side of man's existence. Speak of handkerchiefs in a tragedy? The solecism was as monstrous as picking teeth with a fork.

At a dinner party in Paris not long ago I found myself sitting next to a French Professor of English, who assured me in the course of an otherwise very agreeable conversation that I was a leading member of the Neo-Classic school and that it was as a leading member of the Neo-Classic school that I was lectured about to the advanced students of contemporary English literature under his tutelage. The news depressed me. Classified, like a museum specimen, and lectured about, I felt most dismally posthumous. But that was not all. The thought that I was a Neo-Classic preyed upon my mind—a Neo-Classic without knowing it, a Neo-Classic against all my desires and intentions. For I have never had the smallest ambition to be a Classic of any kind, whether Neo, Palaeo, Proto or Eo. Not at any price. For, to begin with, I have a taste for the lively, the mixed and the incomplete in art, preferring it to the universal and the chemically pure. In the second place, I regard the classical discipline, with its insistence on elimination, concentration, simplification, as being, for all the formal difficulties it imposes on the writer, essentially an escape from, a getting out of, the greatest difficulty—which is to render adequately, in terms of literature, that infinitely complex and mysterious thing, actual reality. The world of mind is a comfortable Wombland, a place to which we flee from the bewildering queerness and multiplicity of the actual world. Matter is incomparably subtler and more intricate than mind. Or, to put it a little more philosophically, the consciousness of events which we have immediately, through our senses and intuitions and feelings, is incomparably subtler than any idea we can subsequently form of that immediate consciousness. Our most refined theories, our most elaborate descriptions are but crude and barbarous simplifications of a reality that is, in every smallest sample, infinitely complex. Now, simplifications must, of course, be made; if they were not, it would be quite impossible to deal artistically (or, for that matter, scientifically) with reality at all. What is the smallest amount of simplification compatible with comprehensibility, compatible with the expression of a humanly significant meaning? It is the business of the non-classical naturalistic writer to discover. His ambition is to render, in literary terms, the quality of immediate experience—in other words, to express the finally inexpressible. To come anywhere near achieving this impossibility is much more difficult, it seems to me, than, by eliminating and simplifying, to achieve the perfectly realizable classical ideal. The cutting out of all the complex particularities of a situation (which means, as we have seen, the cutting out of all that is corporeal in it) strikes me as mere artistic shirking. But I disapprove of the shirking of artistic difficulties. Therefore I find myself disapproving of classicism.

Literature is also philosophy, is also science. In terms of beauty it enunciates truths. The beauty-truths of the best classical works possess, as we have seen, a certain algebraic universality of significance. Naturalistic works contain the more detailed beauty-truths of particular observation. These beauty-truths of art are truly scientific. All that modern psychologists, for example, have done is to systematize and de-beautify the vast treasures of knowledge about the human soul contained in novel, play, poem and essay. Writers like Blake and Shakespeare, like Stendhal and Dostoevsky, still have plenty to teach the modern scientific professional. There is a rich scientific harvest to be reaped in the works even of minor writers. By nature a natural historian, I am ambitious to add my quota to the sum of particularized beauty-truths about man and his relations with the world about him. (Incidentally, this world of relationships, this borderland between 'subjective' and 'objective' is one which literature is peculiarly, perhaps uniquely, well fitted to explore.) I do not want to be a

Classical, or even a Neo-Classical, eliminator and generalizer.

This means, among other things, that I cannot accept the Classicists' excommunication of the body. I think it not only permissible, but necessary, that literature should take cognizance of physiology and should investigate the still obscure relations between the mind and its body. True, many people find the reports of such investigations, when not concealed in scientific textbooks and couched in the decent obscurity of a Graeco-Latin jargon, extremely and inexcusably vulgar; and many more find them downright wicked. I myself have frequently been accused, by reviewers in public and by unprofessional readers in private correspondence, both of vulgarity and of wickedness—on the grounds, so far as I have ever been able to discover, that I reported my investigations into certain phenomena in plain English and in a novel. The fact that many people should be shocked by what he writes practically imposes it as a duty upon the writer to go on shocking them. For those who are shocked by truth are not only stupid, but morally reprehensible as well; the stupid should be educated, the wicked punished and reformed. All these praiseworthy ends can be attained by a course of shocking; retributive pain will be inflicted on the truth-haters by the first shocking truths, whose repetition will gradually

VULGARITY IN LITERATURE 265

build up in those who read them an immunity to pain and will end by reforming and educating the stupid criminals out of their truth-hating. For a familiar truth ceases to shock. To render it familiar is therefore a duty. It is also a pleasure. For, as Baudelaire says, '*ce qu'il y a d'enivrant dans le mauvais goût, c'est le plaisir aristocratique de déplaire.*'

§ v

THE aristocratic pleasure of displeasing is not the only delight that bad taste can yield. One can love a certain kind of vulgarity for its own sake. To overstep artistic restraints, to protest too much for the fun of baroquely protesting—such offences against good taste are intoxicatingly delightful to commit, not because they displease other people (for to the great majority they are rather pleasing than otherwise), but because they are intrinsically vulgar, because the good taste against which they offend is as nearly as possible an absolute good taste; they are artistic offences that have the exciting quality of the sin against the Holy Ghost.

It was Flaubert, I think, who described how he was tempted, as he wrote, by swarms of gaudy images and how, a new St. Antony, he squashed them ruthlessly, like lice, against the bare wall of his study. He was resolved that his work should be adorned only with its own intrinsic beauty and with no extraneous jewels, however lovely in themselves. The saintliness of this ascetic of letters was duly rewarded; there is nothing in all Flaubert's writings that remotely resembles a vulgarity. Those who follow his religion must pray for the strength to imitate their saint. The strength is seldom vouchsafed. The temptations which Flaubert put aside are, by any man of lively fancy and active intellect, incredibly difficult to be resisted. An image presents itself, glittering, iridescent; capture it, pin it down, however irrelevantly too brilliant for its context. A phrase, a situation suggests a whole train of striking or amusing ideas that fly off at a tangent, so to speak, from the round world on which the creator is at work; what an opportunity for saying something witty or profound! True, the ornament will be in the nature of a florid excrescence on the total work; but never mind. In goes the tangent—or rather, out into artistic irrelevancy. And in goes the effective phrase that is too effective, too highly coloured for what it is to express; in goes the too emphatic irony, the too tragical scene, the too pathetic tirade, the too poetical description. If we succumb to all these delightful temptations, if we make welcome all these gaudy lice instead of squashing them at their first appearance, our work will soon glitter like a South

American parvenu, dazzling with parasitic ornament, and vulgar. For a self-conscious artist, there is a most extraordinary pleasure in knowing exactly what the results of showing off and protesting too much must be and then (in spite of this knowledge, or because of it) proceeding, deliberately and with all the skill at his command, to commit precisely those vulgarities, against which his conscience warns him and which he knows he will afterwards regret. To the aristocratic pleasure of displeasing other people, the conscious offender against good taste can add the still more aristocratic pleasure of displeasing himself.

§ VI

EULALIE, Ulalume, Raven and Bells, Conqueror Worm and Haunted Palace. . . . Was Edgar Allan Poe a major poet? It would surely never occur to any English-speaking critic to say so. And yet, in France, from 1850 till the present time, the best poets of each generation—yes, and the best critics, too; for, like most excellent poets, Baudelaire, Mallarmé, Paul Valéry are also admirable critics—have gone out of their way to praise him. Only a year or two ago M. Valéry repeated the now traditional French encomium of Poe, and added at the same time a protest against the faintness of our English praise. We who are speakers of English and not English scholars, who were born into the language and from childhood have been pickled in its literature—we can only say, with all due respect, that Baudelaire, Mallarmé and Valéry are wrong and that Poe is not one of our major poets. A taint of vulgarity spoils, for the English reader, all but two or three of his poems—the marvellous 'City in the Sea' and 'To Helen,' for example, whose beauty and crystal perfection make us realize, as we read them, what a very great artist perished on most of the occasions when Poe wrote verse. It is to this perished artist that the French poets pay their tribute. Not being English they are incapable of appreciating those finer shades of vulgarity that ruin Poe for us, just as we, not being French, are incapable of appreciating those finer shades of lyrical beauty which are, for them, the making of La Fontaine.

The substance of Poe is refined; it is his form that is vulgar. He is, as it were, one of Nature's Gentlemen, unhappily cursed with incorrigible bad taste. To the most sensitive and high-souled man in the world we should find it hard to forgive, shall we say, the wearing of a diamond ring on every finger. Poe does the equivalent of this in his poetry; we notice the solecism and shudder. Foreign observers do not notice it; they detect only the native gentlemanliness in the poetical intention, not the vulgarity in the details of execution. To them,

VULGARITY IN LITERATURE

we seem perversely and quite incomprehensibly unjust.

It is when Poe tries to make it too poetical that his poetry takes on its peculiar tinge of badness. Protesting too much that he is a gentleman, and opulent into the bargain, he falls into vulgarity. Diamond rings on every finger proclaim the parvenu.

Consider, for example, the first two stanzas of 'Ulalume.'

> *The skies they were ashen and sober;*
>   *The leaves they were crisped and sere—*
>   *The leaves they were withering and sere;*
> *It was night in the lonesome October*
>   *Of my most immemorial year;*
> *It was hard by the dim lake of Auber,*
>   *In the misty mid region of Weir—*
> *It was down by the dank tarn of Auber*
>   *In the ghoul-haunted woodland of Weir.*
>
> *Here once, through an alley Titanic,*
>   *Of cypress, I roamed with my soul,*
>   *Of cypress, with Psyche my soul.*
> *These were days when my heart was volcanic*
>   *As the scoriac rivers that roll—*
>   *As the lavas that restlessly roll*
> *Their sulphurous currents down Yaanek*
>   *In the ultimate clime of the pole—*
> *That groan as they roll down Mount Yaanek*
>   *In the realms of the boreal pole.*

These lines protest too much (and with what a variety of voices!) that they are poetical, and, protesting, are therefore vulgar. To start with, the walloping dactylic metre is all too musical. Poetry ought to be musical, but musical with tact, subtly and variously. Metres whose rhythms, as in this case, are strong, insistent and practically invariable offer the poet a kind of short cut to musicality. They provide him (my subject calls for a mixture of metaphors) with a ready-made, reach-me-down music. He does not have to create a music appropriately modulated to his meaning; all he has to do is to shovel the meaning into the moving stream of the metre and allow the current to carry it along on waves that, like those of the best hairdressers, are guaranteed permanent. Many nineteenth-century poets used these metrical short cuts to music, with artistically fatal results.

> *Then when nature around me is smiling*
> *The last smile which answers to mine,*
> *I do not believe it beguiling,*
> *Because it reminds me of thine.*

How can one take even Byron seriously, when he protests his musicalness in such loud and vulgar accents? It is only by luck or an almost superhuman poetical skill that these all too musical metres can be made to sound, through their insistent barrel-organ rhythms,

VULGARITY IN LITERATURE 271

the intricate, personal music of the poet's own meaning. Byron occasionally, for a line or two, takes the hard kink out of those dactylic permanent waves and appears, so to speak, in his own musical hair; and Hood, by an unparalleled prodigy of technique, turns even the reach-me-down music of 'The Bridge of Sighs' into a personal music, made to the measure of the subject and his own emotion. Moore, on the contrary, is always perfectly content with the permanent wave; and Swinburne, that super-Moore of a later generation, was also content to be a permanent waver—the most accomplished, perhaps, in all the history of literature. The complexity of his ready-made musics and his technical skill in varying the number, shape and contour of his permanent waves are simply astonishing. But, like Poe and the others, he protested too much, he tried to be too poetical. However elaborately devious his short cuts to music may be, they are still short cuts—and short cuts (this is the irony) to poetical vulgarity.

A quotation and a parody will illustrate the difference between ready-made music and music made to measure. I remember (I trust correctly) a simile of Milton's:—

> *Like that fair field*
> *Of Enna, where Proserpine gathering flowers,*
> *Herself a fairer flower, by gloomy Dis*
> *Was gathered, which cost Ceres all that pain*
> *To seek her through the world.*

Rearranged according to their musical phrasing, these lines would have to be written thus:—

Like that fair field of Enna,
*   where Proserpine gathering flowers,*
Herself a fairer flower,
*   by gloomy Dis was gathered,*
Which cost Ceres all that pain
To seek her through the world.

The contrast between the lyrical swiftness of the first four phrases, with that row of limping spondees which tells of Ceres' pain, is thrillingly appropriate. Bespoke, the music fits the sense like a glove.

How would Poe have written on the same theme? I have ventured to invent his opening stanza.

It was noon in the fair field of Enna,
* When Proserpina gathering flowers—*
* Herself the most fragrant of flowers,*
Was gathered away to Gehenna
* By the Prince of Plutonian powers;*
Was borne down the windings of Brenner
* To the gloom of his amorous bowers—*
Down the tortuous highway of Brenner
* To the god's agapenonous bowers.*

The parody is not too outrageous to be critically beside the point; and anyhow the music is genuine Poe. That permanent wave is unquestionably an *ondulation de*

VULGARITY IN LITERATURE 273

chez Edgar. The much too musical metre is (to change the metaphor once more) like a rich chasuble, so stiff with gold and gems that it stands unsupported, a carapace of jewelled sound, into which the sense, like some snotty little seminarist, irrelevantly creeps and is lost. This music of Poe's—how much less really musical it is than that which, out of his nearly neutral decasyllables, Milton fashioned on purpose to fit the slender beauty of Proserpine, the strength and swiftness of the ravisher and her mother's heavy, despairing sorrow!

Of the versification of 'The Raven' Poe says, in his *Philosophy of Composition:* 'My first object (as usual) was originality. The extent to which this has been neglected in versification is one of the most unaccountable things in the world. Admitting that there is little possibility of variety in mere *rhythm*, it is still clear that the possible varieties of metre and stanza are absolutely infinite—and yet, *for centuries, no man, in verse, has ever done or ever seemed to think of doing an original thing.*' This fact, which Poe hardly exaggerates, speaks volumes for the good sense of the poets. Feeling that almost all strikingly original metres and stanzas were only illegitimate short cuts to a music which, when reached, turned out to be but a poor and vulgar substitute for individual music, they wisely stuck to the less blatantly musical metres of tradition. The ordinary iambic decasyllable, for example, is intrinsically musical enough to be just able, when required, to stand up by itself. But its musical stiffness can easily be taken out of it. It can be now a chasuble, a golden carapace of sound, now, if the poet so desires, a pliant, soft and, musically speaking, almost neutral material, out of which he can fashion a special music of his own to fit his thoughts and feelings in all their incessant transformations. Good landscape painters seldom choose a 'picturesque' subject; they want to paint their own picture, not have it imposed on them by nature. In the thoroughly paintable little places of this world you will generally find only bad painters. (It's so easy to paint the thoroughly paintable.) The good ones prefer the unspectacular neutralities of the Home Counties to those Cornish coves and Ligurian fishing villages, whose picturesqueness is the delight of all those who have no pictures of their own to project on to the canvas. It is the same with poetry: good poets avoid what I may call, by analogy, 'musicesque' metres, preferring to create their own music out of raw materials as nearly as possible neutral. Only bad poets, or good poets against their better judgment, and by mistake, go to the Musicesque for their material. 'For centuries no man, in verse, has ever done or ever seemed to think of doing an original thing.' It remained for Poe and the other nineteenth-century metrists to do it; Procrustes-like, they tortured and amputated significance into fitting the ready-made music of their highly original metres and stanzas. The result was, in most cases, as vulgar as a Royal Academy Sunrise on Ben Nevis (with Highland Cattle) or a genuine hand-painted sketch of Portofino.

How could a judge so fastidious as Baudelaire listen to Poe's music and remain unaware of its vulgarity? A happy ignorance of English versification preserved him, I fancy, from this realization. His own imitations of mediaeval hymns prove how far he was from understanding the first principles of versification in a language where the stresses are not, as in French, equal, but essentially and insistently uneven. In his Latin poems Baudelaire makes the ghost of Bernard of Cluny write as though he had learned his art from Racine. The principles of English versification are much the same as those of mediaeval Latin. If Baudelaire could discover lines composed of equally stressed syllables in Bernard, he must also have discovered them in Poe. Interpreted according to Racinian principles, such verses as

> *It was down by the dank tarn of Auber*
> *In the ghoul-haunted woodland of Weir*

must have taken on, for Baudelaire, heaven knows what exotic subtlety of rhythm. We can never hope to guess what that ghoul-haunted woodland means to a Frenchman possessing only a distant and theoretical knowledge of our language.

Returning now to 'Ulalume,' we find that its too poetical metre has the effect of vulgarizing by contagion what would be otherwise perfectly harmless and refined technical devices. Thus, even the very mild alliterations in 'the ghoul-haunted woodland of Weir' seem to protest too much. And yet an iambic verse beginning 'Woodland of Weir, ghoul-haunted,' would not sound in the least over-poetical. It is only in the dactylic environment that those two w's strike one as protesting too much.

And then there are the proper names. Well used, proper names can be relied on to produce the most thrilling musical-magical effects. But use them without discretion, and the magic evaporates into abracadabrical absurdity, or becomes its own mocking parody; the over-emphatic music shrills first into vulgarity and finally into ridiculousness. Poe tends to place his proper names in the most conspicuous position in the line (he uses them constantly as rhyme words), showing them off—these magical-musical jewels—as the *rastacouaire* might display the twin cabochon emeralds at his shirt cuffs and the platinum wrist watch, with his monogram in diamonds. These proper-name rhyme-jewels are particularly flashy in Poe's case because they are mostly dissyllabic. Now, the dissyllabic rhyme in English is poetically so precious and so conspicuous by its richness that, if it is not perfect in itself and perfectly used, it emphatically ruins what it was meant emphatically to adorn. Thus, sound and association make of 'Thule' a musical-magical proper name of exceptional power. But when Poe writes,

> *I have reached these lands but newly*
> *From an ultimate dim Thule*,

he spoils the effect which the word ought to produce by insisting too much, and incompetently, on its musicality. He shows off his jewel as conspicuously as he can, but only reveals thereby the badness of its setting and his own Levantine love of display. For 'newly' does not rhyme with 'Thule'—or only rhymes on condition that you pronounce the adverb as though you were a Bengali, or the name as though you came from Whitechapel. The paramour of Goethe's king rhymed perfectly with the name of his kingdom; and when Laforgue wrote of that '*roi de Thulé, Immaculé*' his *rime riche* was entirely above suspicion. Poe's rich rhymes, on the contrary, are seldom above suspicion. That dank tarn of Auber is only very dubiously a fit poetical companion for the tenth month; and though Mount Yaanek is, *ex hypo-*

thesi, a volcano, the rhyme with volcanic is, frankly, impossible. On other occasions Poe's proper names rhyme not only well enough, but actually, in the particular context, much too well. Dead D'Elormie, in 'The Bridal Ballad,' is prosodically in order, because Poe had brought his ancestors over with the Conqueror (as he also imported the ancestors of that Guy de Vere who wept his tear over Lenore) for the express purpose of providing a richly musical-magical rhyme to 'bore me' and 'before me.' Dead D'Elormie is first cousin to Edward Lear's aged Uncle Arly, sitting on a heap of Barley—ludicrous; but also (unlike dear Uncle Arly) horribly vulgar, because of the too musical lusciousness of his invented name and his display, in all tragical seriousness, of an obviously faked Norman pedigree. Dead D'Elormie is a poetical disaster.

§ VII

IT IS vulgar, in literature, to make a display of emotions which you do not naturally have, but think you ought to have, because all the best people do have them. It is also vulgar (and this is the more common case) to have emotions, but to express them so badly, with so many too many protestings, that you seem to have no natural feelings, but to be merely fabricating emotions by a process of literary forgery. Sincerity in art, as I have pointed out elsewhere, is mainly a matter of talent. Keats's love letters ring true, because he had great literary gifts. Most men and women are capable of feeling passion, but not of expressing it; their love letters (as we learn from the specimens read aloud at inquests and murder trials, in the divorce court, during breach of promise cases) are either tritely flat or tritely bombastic. In either case manifestly insincere, and in the second case also vulgar—for to protest too much is always vulgar, when the protestations are so incompetent as not to carry conviction. And perhaps such excessive protestations can never be convincing, however accomplished the protester. D'Annunzio, for example—nobody could do a job of writing better than D'Annunzio. But when, as is too often the case, he makes much ado about nothing, we find it hard to be convinced either of the importance of the nothing, or of the sincerity of the author's emotion about it—and this in spite of the incomparable splendour of D'Annunzio's much ado. True, excessive protestings may convince a certain public at a certain time. But when the circumstances, which rendered the public sensitive to the force and blind to the vulgarity of the too much protesting, have changed, the protests cease to convince. Mackenzie's *Man of Feeling*, for example, protests its author's sensibility with an extravagance that seems now, not merely vulgar, but positively ludicrous. At the time of its publication sentimentality was, for various reasons, extremely fashionable. Circumstances changed and *The Man of Feeling* revealed itself as vulgar to the point of ridiculousness; and vulgar and ridiculous it has remained ever since and doubtless will remain.

Again, to take a more modern instance, circumstances conspired to disguise the fundamental vulgarity of those excessive protestations of humanitarian philanthropy, with which, during the War, M. Romain Rolland filled his pacifist pamphlet. At the time they seemed (it depended on your political convictions) either sublime or diabolically wicked. Circumstances have changed and we are now shocked by the indiscriminateness and unintelligence of M. Rolland's loudly protested universal benevolence. When he said, 'Love your enemies,' Jesus affirmed (he was a realist) that there were enemies to love. M. Rolland's humanitarianism went a step further; there were no enemies, nobody was wrong, nobody deserved condemnation, except perhaps for fighting. There was a general obliteration of distinctions; everything was melted down to the consistency of hog-wash. M. Rolland served out this delicious emotional soup, slop after slop, in generous ladlefuls, of emphatic and undistinguished and therefore eminently unconvincing and vulgar prose. The pamphlet was an infinitely well intentioned and, at the time, a politically valuable performance. But as literature it was vulgar—vulgar, because its excesses of sentiment were quite unbalanced by any excesses of discriminating intelligence; vulgar, because the loud protestings of its manner utterly lacked beauty or elegance. '*Le style c'est l'âme,*' said M. Rolland once, improving (how characteristically!) on the earlier dictum. Papini's comment was unkind: M. Rolland has no style.

Shortly after the War, M. Rolland wrote a novel which was, in its own way and with much less excuse, as vulgar as his war-time pamphlet. I refer to that painful and (in the artistic, not, of course, the moral sense) profoundly 'insincere' book, *Colas Breugnon. Colas Breugnon* is loud with protestations of a positively Rabelaisian jollity. *Malgré tout*, a pacifist can be a good fellow and enjoy his bottle of Burgundy as well as another man. Reading it, one was reminded of those acutely distressing exhibitions of facetiousness and waggish joviality, by means of which certain clergymen try so hard to discount their dog collars and curious waistcoats. Methinks the gentleman doth protest too much, is what we say to ourselves when we have to put up with one of these manifestations of Jocular Christianity. Pantagruelian pacifism is just as distressing, when it fails to come off (for success, I suppose, will justify almost anything) as Jocular Christianity. *Colas Breugnon* failed most lamentably to come off. Its loudly lyrical protestations (so lyrical, that M. Rolland's prose was for ever turning by mistake into blank alexandrines) were simply vulgar. Vulgar, at any rate, for me and, to my knowledge, for several other readers whom, out of self-flattery perhaps, I respect. But I have also met people to whom the too poetical prose and pacifico-pantagruelian protestings of *Colas Breugnon* brought conviction. The vulgarity escaped their notice and they were genuinely moved by what seemed to me, as literature, obviously 'insincere.'

In cases like this one can either shrug one's shoulders and say that there is no accounting for tastes. Or else one can rush in and boldly account for them by invoking, now the influence of special environmental circumstances, now a congenital fatality. The vulgarity of *The Man of Feeling* escaped the notice of most of its readers because, at the time of its publication, sentimentality was, for special historical reasons, more than ordinarily in favour. Similarly there may be, in the environment and history of certain individuals or certain classes, special circumstances which make some kinds of generally recognized vulgarity imperceptible. But there is a natural as well as an acquired blindness to vulgarity. The Brahmins of the critical hierarchy are sensitive to differences of shade and tone which, among the Sudras, pass quite unnoticed. Needless to say, each one of us conceives that his place is among the Brahmins. I shall make, as a matter of course, the universal assumption—justifiably, in the circumstances; for a critic cannot do his business unless he first assumes that he is right; righter than any one else, or than a few specifically excepted judges. Having made this assumption, I am entitled to affirm that all those who do not agree with me (and with those who think like me) about the vulgarity of a given work are members of a lower caste in the critical hierarchy—that is, unless they can invoke as their excuse for judging badly the pressure of special external circumstances. Here I may speak without irrelevance of that curious dulness of perception, that lack of discrimination displayed, as every critic must have had many opportunities of amazedly discovering, by even apparently intelligent readers, not to mention all the others. Because we all know how to read, we imagine that we know what we read. Enormous fallacy! In reality, I imagine, the gift of literary discrimination is at least as rare as that of musical discrimination. We admit quite cheerfully the truth about music. But if music were not an educational luxury; if every child were taught its notes as now it is taught its letters, if piano playing were, like geometry and French grammar, a compulsory subject in every school curriculum, what then? Should we as easily admit our lack of musical discrimination as we do at present, when most of us have never learned to read a simple melody or play on any instrument? I think not. Knowing something about the technique of music, we should imagine that we knew something (or, more probably, that we knew everything) about its substance. Anyhow, this is what seems to have happened in the case of literature. Because we have spent some years in acquiring the art of reading books, we think we have acquired the art of judging them. But in spite of universal education, there are still vast numbers of people who spontaneously love the lowest when they read it, and a great many more who, loving the highest, also love, if not the lowest, at any rate the low and the middling with an equal and quiet undiscriminating enthusiasm. To a sensitive critic the judgments passed on books by quite intelligent and highly educated people often seem bewildering in their irrelevance and apparent perversity. He hears them speaking of utterly dissimilar works, as though there were nothing to choose between them. One happens to be refined and another vulgar; one genuine and another manifestly a fraud and a forgery. But such trifling differences seem to pass quite unnoticed. There

VULGARITY IN LITERATURE 285

are men, I suppose, who find it hard to distinguish between a dog and a toasting fork; but one seldom meets them, because they are almost all in asylums. But men who fail to distinguish between works of art which, for the sensitive critic, are at least as dissimilar as dogs and toasting forks, run no risk of being certified as insane. On the contrary, they seem to be destined, in most cases, to become either the Head Masters of our most splendid Public Schools, or else Prime Ministers.

Even the greatest writers (to return to our original theme) can be guilty on occasion of the most shocking emotional vulgarity. Balzac and Dickens will provide us, in *Séraphita* and *The Old Curiosity Shop*, with striking examples of various kinds of this vulgarity.

Séraphita is the most considerable work in that section of the Human Comedy devoted to religion in general and in particular (for Balzac was always specially interested in mysticism) to mystical religion. 'Mysticism? What you mean is misty schism,' was the remark once made to a friend of mine (who moves, as I, alas, do not, in the highest ecclesiastical circles) by a more than ordinarily eminent Eminence. The pun is not a bad one and, like the best Irish bulls, is pregnant. For the literature of mysticism, which is a literature about the inexpressible, is for the most part misty indeed—a London fog, but coloured pink. It is only in the works of the very best mystical writers that the fog lifts—to reveal what? A strange alternation of light and darkness: light to the limits of the possibly illuminable and after that the darkness of paradox and incomprehensibility, or the yet deeper, the absolute night of silence. So much for the mist. As for the schism, that has always had a tendency to open its gulfs round the feet of the Catholic mystics. The Church has, at all times and very naturally, felt suspicious of those who insist on approaching God directly and not through the official ecclesiastical channels. And, strong in their immediate knowledge of God, the mystics on their side have often had a very short way with dogmas, rites and the priesthood. Mysticism brings with it the decay of authority. The process is, to some extent at least, reversible; the decay of authority leads to mysticism. For whenever, thanks to the growth of scepticism, dogmas have come to be unbelievable and priesthood has lost its magical prestige, then mysticism comes into its own—into its own, at any rate, as a philosophical theory, though not necessarily as a practical way of life. Mystical religion is the ideal religion for doubters—those ultimate schismatics who have separated themselves from all belief. For the mystic is dispensed from intellectually *believing* in God; he *feels* God. Or, to put it more accurately, he has (in Professor Otto's phrase) a 'numinous' emotion, which he is at liberty to rationalize into a theological dogma—or not to rationalize, according to taste; for it is perfectly possible to have a numinous emotion without believing in the existence of a *numen*, or divinity, as its hypothetical cause.

Contemporary scepticism is tempered with the usual superstitions—belief in ghosts, preoccupation with magic and the like—and also with an interest in mysticism. In some cases this interest finds a practical expression. But as the practice of mystical religion entails the practice of asceticism, and as asceticism is not popular in this mass-producing age, when the first duty of every good citizen is to consume as much as he possibly can, our interest in mysticism is mainly theoretical and scientific.

It is painfully easy for a sceptic, who is also an amateur, theoretical and non-practising mystic, to fall into artistic insincerity, when writing about the kind of religious experiences which interest him. For to write convincingly about things which you do not know at first hand is very hard. The temptation is always to make up for deficiency of knowledge by stylistic emphasis and redundancy, by protesting too much. Only those who write consummately well can hope, in such circumstances, to avoid insincerity and vulgarity.

Balzac had nearly all the gifts. Two only were lacking

—the gift of writing well and the gift of mysticism (in the mistiest and most schismatic as well as the most definite sense of the word). This was the more unfortunate, as he chose writing as his profession and mysticism as the subject of much of his writing.

Wherever he is dealing with subjects of which he has a natural first-hand knowledge, we do not notice the defects in Balzac's prose. In fact, it is not defective. It is only in cases where he doesn't really know what he is talking about that Balzac's defects as a stylist emerge and become distressingly manifest. For in these cases he protests too much—with fatal results.

Balzac, I think, was less of a natural mystic than almost any other great writer. He had a prodigious intuitive knowledge of man as a social animal, of man in his mundane relations with other men. But of man in solitude, man in his relations with the universe and those mysterious depths within himself—in a word, of man the mystical animal—he knew, personally and at first hand, very little. I remember one day saying something of this kind to D. H. Lawrence, who nodded his agreement with me and summed up the matter by saying that Balzac was 'a gigantic dwarf.' A gigantic dwarf—gigantic in his power of understanding and vividly re-creating every conceivable worldly activity, with all the thoughts and feelings that the world can give birth to in a human mind; but dwarfish when it came to dealing artistically with those inner activities which fill the mind when a man is living in solitude, or else—a naked individuality—in unworldly relationship with the naked individuality of other human beings. Dwarfish, in a word, precisely in those respects in which Lawrence himself was gigantic; and gigantic in a sphere where Lawrence, the most unworldly of writers, did not exist, did not even want to exist.

Religion and, in its widest, mistiest sense, mysticism have an important place in human life. Ambitious to make his Comedy complete, Balzac gave them an important place in his work. Besides, he had the true romantic feeling for chiaroscuro. He loved to bring together, in picturesque contrast, this world with the heaven of idealism, angels with villainous Du Tillys and Nucingens, ambitious Rastignacs with utterly disinterested sages, artists and saints. Indeed, if there had been no such thing as mysticism, Balzac would have been compelled by his artistic principles to invent it; for that colossal statue of Mammon in his pantheon demanded urgently as pendant and foil a no less colossal statue of Idealism to fill the vacant niche on the opposite side of the aisle. Unhappily for Balzac's reputation as a religious writer, mysticism exists, and with it a considerable body of mystical literature, good, bad and indifferent. There are standards by which to judge such works as *Séraphita* and *Louis Lambert*. Judged by those standards, Balzac's mysticism turns out to be a very poor and at the same time (and for that very reason) a very pretentious thing. '*Quelle froide plaisanterie!*' was his Don Juan's summing up of the universe; and this, I believe, was what the essential Balzac naturally and intuitively felt about the whole business. Perhaps—his own temperament being more sanguine than Don Juan's—he would have found the pleasantry warm rather than cold; but, whatever its temperature, it was always a joke, huge, bad and rather malicious. On to this natural cynicism Balzac grafted, by a process and as the result of reflection, ideals, religion, angels, Swedenborg—what not? But it is significant that whenever he wrote of these things, he wrote, as Blake declared that Milton wrote of God, 'in chains' (elastic chains; for they allowed him to kick and gesticulate most violently); and that whenever he wrote on a theme, which allowed him to give expression to his high-spirited natural cynicism, he wrote at ease and, relatively, very well.

Fashion, no doubt, as well as philosophy and an ambition to achieve universality, had an influence in turning Balzac, in spite of his temperament, towards mysticism. He lived in that strange age of Catholic reaction, when smart young men about town would go to the Abbé Dupanloup to study their Catechism and when, in the phrase of Joseph de Maistre, irreligion was *canaille*. Making a pleasure as well as a virtue of political necessity, Balzac's contemporaries used the restored religion as a source of emotional excitement. Not seriously believing (it was difficult at the beginning of the nineteenth century to do that), they went to church for the sake of the aesthetic and 'numinous' thrills which it could provide. To use the modern jargon, they were interested in religious experience, not in religious dogmas, which they made use of simply to procure the pleasant experiences. (Thus, an intellectual belief in the existence of a God now loving and now angry can be made to yield delicious thrills alternately of confidence and terror.) Balzac was 'in the movement'—but, as usual, moving much faster and more violently than the current which bore him along. By nature a high-spirited cynic and sceptic (*plus il vit, plus il douta*), he could transform himself on occasion, by sheer force of make-believe, into a fashionable church-goer, a more than fashionable Swedenborgian. The superstitiousness natural to all sceptics (for to a Pyrrhonist absolutely everything is possible) came to his assistance here. Besides, like most great men, he was a bit of a charlatan; he loved to impress his readers, he loved to tell them the answer to the Riddle of the Universe—straight from the horse's mouth, so to speak. (For a philosophic tipster, Swedenborg and Boehme are obviously winners.) Finally, Balzac possessed the intelligent literary man's interest in science—that quite irresponsible interest of the man who has never had any scientific training, never done any practical scientific work and for whom, in consequence, science is just a magic art, like any other, only more respectable, guaranteed as it is by sorcerers who have received knighthoods and rosettes of the Legion of Honour. Nor does the intelligent literary man much distinguish one scientist from another; the only preferences he has are for those scientists he can understand and those who deal with the kind of subject that lends itself to literary treatment. Which generally means, in practice, that he prefers bad scientists to good ones. In Balzac's day the literary man's favourite scientist was not Laplace or Faraday, but Mesmer— just as to-day it is to the wilder Freudians rather than to Einstein or Pavlov that he turns. Science—the science of the intelligent literary man—seems to confirm the misty and schismatical doctrines of mysticism. Which, for Balzac, was a further justification, if any were needed, for feeling, or trying to feel, or at any rate saying that one felt those mystical emotions which all the best people, from the *ultra* duchess with her *six cent*

VULGARITY IN LITERATURE 293

mille livres de rente down to the humblest saint in the calendar, were feeling or had felt.

I have lingered thus long over Balzac, because I feel his case to be so instructive, so profoundly relevant. He set himself the task of reviving in the person of the novelist that man of universal learning, that creator-of-all-trades, who was the glory of the Renaissance. His ambition was to know everything, both in the outer world and in that within; to know everything and to be every one—yes, to be both mystic and mundane, idealist as well as cynic, contemplator no less than man of action. That he should have realized even a part of this immense and impossible ambition is a sign of his extraordinary power. His problems are the problems which confront the contemporary novelist who aspires, not indeed to universality (for only a lunatic or a conscious superman could cherish such ambitions to-day) but, more modestly, to intelligence, to awareness of contemporaneity, to self-consciousness, to truthfulness, to artistic integrity. And the temptations by which Balzac was beset, the dangers which threatened and the artistic disasters which overtook him are precisely the temptations, dangers and disasters, in the midst of which the contemporary novelist must, if he is in the least ambitious, pick his way.

In *Séraphita* we see a terrifying example of the disaster which overtakes writers who succumb to the temptation of protesting too much about matters of which they know too little. (I use the word 'know' to signify, in this case, the immediate, first-hand knowledge that is born of feeling. Balzac had a considerable abstract knowledge of mysticism; it was his crime that he also pretended to possess an intuitive, emotional knowledge from within, and his misfortune that he lacked, or lost, those literary arts, by means of which he might have made the pretence convincing. 'Lost'—for, as I have said, Balzac could write, not beautifully perhaps, but well and vigorously enough about his beloved World, just as Milton could be unaffectedly sublime about the Flesh (his account of the first wedding is bright with an almost unearthly glow of sensuality) and that indomitable Devil, whose self-esteem was founded, like Milton's own, on 'just and right.' The moment Balzac had to protest too much, as he had to do about matters which did not lie near his heart, he lost this power to write well and sank or soared into fustian.

Séraphita is characterized by a peculiar emotional vulgarity. In his attempt to express the mystical emotions which he does not naturally have, Balzac is forced to make incessant overstatements. Not only do the characters themselves protest, both in speech and in action, much too much; the symbols with which Balzac surrounds them also protest too much. It would be easy by means of extended quotation to illustrate what I have been saying about *Séraphita*. But world and time are lacking, and I must be content to cite this one sentence, into which Balzac has considerately crammed examples of almost all the faults which characterize his mystical writing. 'And with a lifted finger, this singular being showed her the blue aureole which the clouds, by leaving a clear space above their heads, had drawn in the sky and in which the stars could be seen in daylight, in virtue of hitherto unexplained atmospheric laws.' In these few lines Balzac has succumbed to three separate temptations. First, in his anxiety to impress us with the mystical merits of his Séraphita, he has called her 'a singular being.' (He gives her many other such honorific titles in the course of his narrative: she is 'unique,' 'inexplicable,' and the like.) The adjective protests too much about a matter which it was the business of the story itself and not the commenting author to make clear.

Consider, in the second place, that aureole of blue sky, which follows Séraphita about in all her rambles like a celestial dog, however cloudy the weather. This symbol is so obviously poetical, so loudly significant of Higher Things, that it fails to impress—it merely shocks, as the diamond rings symbolical of Levantine opulence merely shock without impressing. The stars are just a set of diamond studs to match the rings. But in those hitherto unexplained atmospheric laws, in virtue of which they are visible by daylight, we have another, quite new vulgarity—an intellectual vulgarity this time. It is Balzac the charlatan, Balzac the philosophic tipster giving us a piece of inside information, straight from the scientific horse's mouth. Now one can talk very knowingly in a novel, poem or other work of literary art even about such things as hitherto unexplained atmospheric laws, without necessarily being vulgar; but only on condition that the talking is done tactfully and with perfect relevance. One must be, as Jean Coteau said of that most universally knowing of modern novelists, M. Paul Morand, '*un nouveau riche qui sait recevoir.*' M. Morand has a wonderfully airy, easy way of implying that he has looked into everything—absolutely everything, from God and the Quantum Theory to the slums of Baku (the world's most classy slums—didn't you know it?), from the Vanderbilt family and all the Ritz Hotels to the unpublished poetry of Father Hopkins. Just the quick passing implication of knowledge, just the right word in each particular case, the absolutely correct, esoteric formula —that is all. M. Morand is the almost perfect literary knower; he hardly ever, at any rate in his earlier books, makes a mistake. Balzac was too serious in his charlatanism, too vastly ambitious, too energetic to be a very tactful intellectual hostess; for all his wealth he did not know how to receive. Thus, in the present case, he has fallen into vulgarity, because he could not resist the temptation of being knowing at a most inopportune moment. That horse's-mouth information about atmospheric laws has been dragged irrelevantly and absurdly into the middle of a poetic symbol—a much too poetic symbol, as we have seen; which only makes the incongruity more apparent. Blue aureoles are a part of an angel's uniform, as much *de rigueur* among Cherubs as top-hats at a Royal Garden Party. Unexplained atmospheric laws have nothing to do with angels. By bringing them thus incongruously together, Balzac calls attention to the vulgarity of a knowingness which insists on displaying itself at all costs and on all occasions.

The case of Dickens is a strange one. The really monstrous emotional vulgarity, of which he is guilty now and then in all his books and almost continuously in *The Old Curiosity Shop*, is not the emotional vulgarity of one who simulates feelings which he does not have. It is evident, on the contrary, that Dickens felt most poignantly for and with his Little Nell; that he wept over her sufferings, piously revered her goodness and exulted in her joys. He had an overflowing heart; but the trouble was that it overflowed with such curious and even rather repellent secretions. The creator of the later Pickwick and the Cheeryble Brothers, of Tim Linkinwater the bachelor and Mr. Garland and so many other gruesome old Peter Pans was obviously a little abnormal in his emotional reactions. There was something rather wrong with a man who could take this lachrymose and tremulous pleasure in adult infantility. He would doubtless have justified his rather frightful emotional taste by a reference to the New Testament. But the child-like qualities of character commended by Jesus are certainly not the same as those which distinguish the old infants in Dickens's novels. There is all the difference in the world between infants and children. Infants are stupid and unaware and subhuman. Children are remarkable for their intelligence and ardour, for their curiosity, their intolerance of shams, the clarity and ruthlessness of their vision. From all accounts Jesus must have been child-like, not at all infantile. A child-like man is not a man whose development has been arrested; on the contrary, he is a man who has given himself a chance of continuing to develop long after most adults have muffled themselves in the cocoon of middle-aged habit and convention. An infantile man is one who has not developed at all, or who has regressed towards the womb, into a comfortable unawareness. So far from being attractive and commendable, an infantile man is really a most repulsive, because a truly monstrous and misshapen, being. A writer who can tearfully adore these stout or cadaverous old babies, snugly ensconced in their mental and economic womb-substitutes and sucking, between false teeth, their thumbs, must have something seriously amiss with his emotional constitution.

One of Dickens's most striking peculiarities is that, whenever in his writing he becomes emotional, he ceases instantly to use his intelligence. The overflowing of his heart drowns his head and even dims his eyes; for, whenever he is in the melting mood, Dickens ceases to be able and probably ceases even to wish to see reality. His one and only desire on these occasions is just to overflow, nothing else. Which he does, with a vengeance and in an atrocious blank verse that is meant to be poetical prose and succeeds only in being the worst kind of fustian. 'When Death strikes down the innocent and young, from every fragile form from which he lets the panting spirit free, a hundred virtues rise, in shapes of mercy, charity and love, to walk the world and bless it. Of every tear that sorrowing mortals shed on such green graves, some good is born, some gentler nature comes. In the Destroyer's steps there spring up bright creations that defy his power, and his dark path becomes a way of light to Heaven.' And so on, a stanchless flux.

Mentally drowned and blinded by the sticky overflowings of his heart, Dickens was incapable, when moved, of re-creating, in terms of art, the reality which had moved him, was even, it would seem, unable to perceive that reality. Little Nelly's sufferings and death distressed him as, in real life, they would distress any normally constituted man; for the suffering and death of children raise the problem of evil in its most unanswerable form. It was Dickens's business as a writer to re-create in terms of his art this distressing reality. He failed. The history of Little Nell is distressing indeed, but not as Dickens presumably meant it to be distressing; it is distressing in its ineptitude and vulgar sentimentality.

A child, Ilusha, suffers and dies in Dostoevsky's *Brothers Karamazov*. Why is this history so agonizingly moving, when the tale of Little Nell leaves us not merely cold, but derisive? Comparing the two stories, we are instantly struck by the incomparably greater richness in factual detail of Dostoevsky's creation. Feeling did not prevent him from seeing and recording, or rather re-creating. All that happened round Ilusha's deathbed he saw, unerringly. The emotion-blinded Dickens noticed practically nothing of what went on in Little Nelly's neighbourhood during the child's last days. We are almost forced, indeed, to believe that he didn't want to see anything. He wanted to be unaware himself and he wanted his readers to be unaware of everything except Little Nell's sufferings on the one hand and her goodness and innocence on the other. But goodness and innocence and the undeservedness of suffering and even, to some extent, suffering itself are only significant in relation to the actual realities of human life. Isolated, they cease to mean anything, perhaps to exist. Even the classical writers surrounded their abstract and algebraical personages with at least the abstract and algebraical implication of the human realities, in relation to which virtues and vices are significant. Thanks to Dickens's pathologically deliberate unawareness, Nell's virtues are marooned, as it were, in the midst of a boundless waste of unreality; isolated, they fade and die. Even her sufferings and death lack significance because of this isolation. Dickens's unawareness was the death of death itself. Unawareness, according to he ethics of Buddhism, is one of the deadly sins. The stupid are wicked. (Incidentally, the cleverest men can, sometimes and in certain circumstances, reveal themselves as profoundly

—criminally—stupid. You can be an acute logician and at the same time an emotional cretin.) Damned in the realm of conduct, the unaware are also damned aesthetically. Their art is bad; instead of creating, they murder.

Art, as I have said, is also philosophy, is also science. Other things being equal, the work of art which in its own way 'says' more about the universe will be better than the work of art which says less. (The 'other things' which have to be equal are the forms of beauty, in terms of which the artist must express his philosophic and scientific truths.) Why is *The Rosary* a less admirable novel than *The Brothers Karamazov?* Because the amount of experience of all kinds understood, 'felt into,' as the Germans would say, and artistically re-created by Mrs. Barclay is small in comparison with that which Dostoevsky feelingly comprehended and knew so consummately well how to re-create in terms of the novelist's art. Dostoevsky covers all Mrs. Barclay's ground and a vast area beside. The pathetic parts of *The Old Curiosity Shop* are as poor in understood and artistically re-created experience as *The Rosary*—indeed, I think they are even poorer. At the same time they are vulgar (which *The Rosary*, that genuine masterpiece of the servants' hall, is not). They are vulgar, because their poverty is a pretentious poverty, because their disease (for the quality of Dickens's sentimentality is truly pathological) professes to be the most radiant health; because they protest their unintelligence, their lack of understanding with a vehemence of florid utterance that is not only shocking, but ludicrous.